My Struggle, His Glory

Compiled by Boyd Deal
Edited by Jessica Ingram

ISBN: 9781076923684

Second Chance Ministries
mysecondchancestory@gmail.com
P.O. Box 533
Ariton, Alabama 36311
mysecondchancestory.wixsite.com/hope

DEDICATION

To all the people that contributed stories, thank you for sharing your personal struggle so that others may see God's love, mercy, and grace. Your contributions transformed this project from an idea into a book. God planted a seed in my heart to write a book and your willingness to share your story was the thing that made that seed grow.

To Leah, you are my biggest supporter and encourager. I am very grateful that God brought you into my life. God used you to heal me from one of my biggest struggles in life. If I could have a "do over", I would still choose you.

To Bradley and Tyler, when I count my blessings, you are at the top of the list. God has blessed me in so many ways, but no gift has been better than being able to call you my son.

To the rest of my family and friends, this project has taken time away from all of you but you have never questioned my reason for pursuing it. Thank you for your support, encouragement and prayers. I love each of you.

Boyd

CONTENTS

ACKNOWLEDGEMENTS

By Boyd Deal

First and foremost, I want to thank God for giving me the opportunity to write this book. I have prayed daily for His guidance and I believe His hands have directed my path every step of the way. I pray He is satisfied with my effort.

To Leah, Bradley, Tyler, Mackenzie, and Buck: Thank you for your loving, encouraging, and supportive spirits. This book project has been one of the most challenging and rewarding things I have ever attempted to do. Soliciting, writing, and editing the stories has taken a lot of my time and energy away from you. However, I am confident you understand why I was being obedient to God.

To my college and career Sunday school class at Ariton Baptist Church: Thank you for allowing me to lead your class for six years. You challenged, motivated, and encouraged me to pursue God's calling. You are servants and leaders. I can't wait to see how God will continue to use you to do His work and to spread His message.

To Maggie Walsh: Thank you for guiding me in the right direction so I could pursue this book project.

To Jessica Ingram, my editor: Thank you for transforming this project from an idea to a book. You have worked extremely hard to make this successful, and I will always be grateful for your contributions. Your leadership and knowledge has been invaluable.

To Brittany Logan, Mackenzie Deal, Charlene Martin, and Leah Deal: Thank you for your assistance editing the stories. You have spent many hours helping me complete God's calling.

To Laura Unger: Thank you for using your gift of creativity to design the cover for the book. You took my thoughts and changed them into a beautiful piece of art.

Last, but certainly not least, I want to thank each person that allowed me to use their story for this book. I have been overwhelmed by the way you have shared your struggles, feelings, and emotions. It is easy to see each of you have suffered during a season of your life, but due to God's redemption, love, mercy, and grace you are now able to praise Him for His blessings.

INTRODUCTION

By Boyd Deal

My Struggle, His Glory contains testimonies from forty different people. Instead of writing the book only about my own personal struggles, I have solicited help from different people so they can share about their struggles, too. This allowed me to include a greater number of struggles that people endure. Their stories show God's redemption, love, mercy, and grace. Their testimonies show how God brought them through the worst times of their lives and how they are able to praise God for what He has done in their lives. Even though every story involves a personal struggle, they all have two other common themes: hope and praise.

When you read each story, I hope you can feel the pain and suffering they have endured. But, more importantly, I hope you can also see the way God has redeemed them from the worst times in their lives.

My goal for writing *My Struggle, His Glory* is to allow Christians to use their personal struggles to be messengers of hope, encouragement, and faith for those going through a difficult time. I want people to know God is with them even when they may not feel His presence.

My heart breaks for all of the people who are struggling in life. I am also deeply concerned over the number of suicides that occur locally and nationally. Unfortunately, this appears to be a growing trend among people going through a personal struggle.

It is hard for some people to imagine what it feels like to be hopeless, alone, or desperate. I know that pain. I know what it feels like to travel through a valley. I lost my dad when I was ten years old. I went through a divorce when I was twenty-five years old. Each of these events left me feeling like my life may never have any value or purpose. However, now I can see how God brought me through each situation, and how each event forced me to rely on God's strength and not on my own strength. Everything I have been able to overcome and accomplish is because of God.

It took me a long time, but now I understand how God can use the painful events in my life to make me a better person. I will always thank

Him and praise Him for getting me through those dark seasons of my life.

No one is immune from facing hardships or challenges. This includes the wealthy, celebrities, pastors, and, yes, even you. Have your concerns taken God's place in your life? In the middle of a storm you can panic and give up hope, or you can give your burdens to God and pray for His mercy, grace, and healing. At times the road is difficult, but you are not alone. You may suffer now, but your reward awaits you. We have hope and faith because of the promises God has given us.

After reading the personal testimonies in this book, I hope and pray the people struggling will find a reason to praise and worship God. I pray that this book will help change someone's life. Hopefully, it will be your life that is changed. I hope God will use you to encourage and strengthen others in a way you never thought was possible. You, too, can be God's instrument of hope. Are you willing to do whatever He asks and go wherever He leads you?

Sometimes we experience an event or series of events in life that can change our thoughts, goals, decisions, and priorities. Even at your lowest point, God has a plan for your life that is greater than anything you can imagine.

I have discovered that obedience requires faith and courage. God has led me down a path that I never thought I would travel. After a few years of running from God's calling to write a book, I am now sprinting towards Him with everything I have to give. Even though I do not feel worthy, I am submitting to God so I can do His will.

What will be your testimony? It may involve how you recovered from some type of hardship or loss, and how you are able to glorify God for getting you through it. It may be the one thing that helps someone else trust God and rely on Him for strength.

Your greatest accomplishment in life may not be what you do, but what God does through someone else because of you.

How will you be remembered?

JESSE

By Barbara Anderson

It was a beautiful Thursday morning in September that started like most others. I prepared for work without a burden or care in sight. Well, other than competing with my husband, Johnny, for the one shower in our home.

I was fighting the clock as I prepared for work. I was also trying to get a jump on a birthday meal for our youngest son, Joshua, who lived a short distance from us. His older brother, Jesse, who lived in Auburn, Alabama, had invited him up for the weekend. Jesse had purchased Auburn vs Arkansas State football tickets so they could attend the game together on Saturday.

I scurried out the door and into my car heading to my job as a surgical nurse. My car radio was tuned to my favorite Christian radio station. I was happy and singing along. I saw it as an opportunity to offer up my small gift of praise and worship to God for the twenty minutes that it would take me to get to work.

I crossed the four-lane highway that morning and turned onto the road that would take me to my destination. But this morning was different. In my rearview mirror, God had positioned the sunrise in such a precise manner that the view totally took my breath away. The Bible says in Psalm 19:1 that even the heavens declare the glory of God. This morning I was privileged to have a front row seat even if it meant I was looking in the rearview mirror.

I was in the presence of Jehovah, and His peace was so surreal. I talked to Him as though He was a physical passenger in my car. I told Him I loved Him. I thanked Him for the blessings in my life that were so undeserved. I thanked Him for His mercy. I thanked Him for my family. I told Him, "Father, You are so good to me all the time."

He replied back in that small still voice that I remember today with this question: "Am I good all the time?"

I said, "Yes Lord, You are good all the time." Then came His second question, "Am I still good in the bad times?"

3

Still focusing on the masterpiece of the sunrise, I responded, "Yes Lord. You are still God, and You are still good even in the bad times." In less than two hours I would come face to face with those questions once again.

As I clocked in at work, I quickly checked the schedule and hurried to my designated area to prepare for the day. My first patient was a pediatric patient with severe Down Syndrome.

Normally, I would never carry my personal phone into the operating room, but for whatever reason, I did this morning. Towards the end of this baby's surgery I heard my phone ring from the desk where I had stored it. Not recognizing the number I quickly dismissed it, which I would later regret. Within a matter of minutes I received an overhead page.

One of my coworkers said with a tone of urgency, "Barbara, it's your husband. It's an emergency. He needs to speak to you now."

My first thoughts were that something had happened to one of our elderly parents. With his voice shaking and frantic, he blurted out that I needed to come home immediately. Jesse had been involved in a motorcycle accident and had been flown to the trauma center in Columbus, Georgia. Our presence was requested as soon as possible. Our other son, Joshua, would meet us at the hospital. That three-hour drive seemed like an eternity. Few words were spoken between us.

My husband had received specific instructions from the hospital liaison in regards to where and what we needed to do upon arrival. We were met by a kind and compassionate woman, whom I later learned was designated to handle the trauma cases. She made a phone call and we were ushered to the critical care floor.

Upon arrival there, we identified ourselves and were quickly ushered by two neurotrauma surgeons into a private conference room. Reaching out and holding my hand, one doctor uttered four words that would forever change the entire course of our lives: "There is no hope."

Author and minister Charles Swindoll said, "We can live forty days without food, eight days without water, four minutes without air, but only a few seconds without hope."

We were told that Jesse was on life support. Upon impact with a truck his helmet came off and he suffered massive head injuries. There was no hope; he was going to die. Those words are a parent's worst nightmare. No hope.

The atmosphere as we sat by Jesse's bedside was heavy and dark. We sat in a state of shock, disbelief, and confusion. How could this be happening to us?

As a nurse I was taught that hearing can be the last thing a dying patient loses. We told Jesse we were there with him and that he was not alone. We told him how much we loved him. We pleaded with him to fight death and stay with us. The only response came from the ventilator at his bedside, the cardiac monitor above his bed, and the chirping of the numerous infusions going into his body. How could a day that started out so peaceful and perfect, filled with God's presence so surreal, end up like this? End up with our family being catapulted into such a massive storm where there seemed to be no hope or chance of survival for any of us? Though we were not declared clinically dead like Jesse, the three of us were dying on the inside just the same.

I cried out to God. I pleaded with God. I begged God to spare my son's life. I even tried to bargain with God. I reminded God of my faith in Him. I remember telling God that I knew beyond a shadow of doubt, in spite of the medical diagnoses, He could heal our son. He could raise him up perfect and whole, and the four of us could walk out of the hospital. I've never tried to barter with God like that before. I've never had a reason.

I am married to a godly, Christian man who loves the Lord with all his heart and served as a minister of music long before we were married. Johnny is my rock and has such unshakeable faith. Music has always filled our home and as our boys grew up, they embraced the love of music too.

Over the years, when I was too busy to listen for the voice of God, He would use some song at just the right time to speak to me. Johnny, being the head of our home, ensured a godly foundation for all of us, but this time when I looked at my husband I saw a man broken beyond words, asking God, "Why?"

Within hours, news of our tragedy had flooded cell phones and Facebook pages. The hospital was filling up with our family and friends who filtered in and out of Jesse's room.

I felt like I had literally stepped outside of my body. The tears came. I cried and cried. I continued to plead for Jesse's life over the following hours.

The memory of my early morning drive flooded my mind like a dam had suddenly broken up river.

Again I said, "Yes Father, You are good all the time."

The still, small voice responded with a question: "Barbara, do you trust Me?"

"Yes, Father, I do," I replied.

"Then ask Me for My perfect will to be done in Jesse's life."

That was by far the hardest prayer I have ever prayed in my entire life. It scared me and I felt physically sick all over. My chest hurt. The physical, emotional, and mental pain was driving me to a breaking point. All I could say was "Jesus." I felt so alone, in spite of being surrounded by family and friends.

I stood at the window in his hospital room and saw a beautiful sunset. But unlike the sunrise I had witnessed earlier that day, I felt no peace or comfort in it. I thought about how my son would never witness another sunrise or sunset. My heart was breaking and nothing could be done to change anything.

The next day would be Joshua's birthday. Over the years, after battling for bikes and baseball gloves, our boys had grown from just being brothers to best friends. I prayed silently that Joshua's birthday would not be marred with his brother's death.

There is a song that says, "I'm not skilled to understand what God has willed, what God has planned. I only know at His right hand stands One who is my Savior."

Jesse died early the next morning on Joshua's birthday with his family at his bedside. I saw the sunrise through Jesse's hospital window and thought just how truly fragile and short life is, and how everything can change in a blink of an eye.

For me, there has been no "moving on" after Jesse's death, only "moving with." I have come to realize that time doesn't necessarily heal all wounds, but Jesus does.

There are so many things I don't know the answers to, but it has been during this period of immeasurable brokenness that I rediscovered the character of God. He has shown Himself to be so faithful to me.

I wish I had answers for a believer's grief, but I don't. I stand firm on the truths that are found in the Bible. He has taught me that He will bring good out of our worst hurts and tragedies, which included the death of our son, Jesse. Psalm 34:18 says, "The Lord is close to the brokenhearted and saves those who are crushed in spirit."

It was during the darkest period of my life that Jesus became so very real to me. I experienced a renewed faith, trust, and hope while walking this horrible road of loss.

I also experienced a very dark and angry time for several months following Jesse's death.

I asked God more questions than I received answers for. It was during this time He reminded me that He too lost His son. The difference was that the mercy He showered on Jesse was not shown to His own Son, the Son who would bear the sins of the world. Jesse's death was fast and instant. Jesse was clinically dead at the scene because of his injuries.

Jesse did not suffer. But Jesus was stripped and beaten. A crown of thorns was shoved on His head. He was spit on, had His beard pulled out, and was nailed to a cross. He did not die instantly or painlessly. He was well aware of what was happening.

Then, God reminded me of another aspect I hadn't thought much about until Jesse's accident. I stayed at Jesse's bedside throughout the entire ordeal. I refused to leave him until the funeral home came to transport his body. He was well cared for throughout the entire ordeal. The Bible says that Mary was with her son also.

I cannot begin to describe how at that instant my heart started grieving for Mary. As a mother, I can only imagine the horrible ordeal she endured as she witnessed this barbaric event unfolding right before her eyes. Jesus felt every bit of the pain being inflicted on His body. Surely He must have cried out during His suffering. It was then I realized that God had shown to me His loving kindness and mercy.

God's victory over death makes it possible for us to grieve with hope. The Bible says because of my profession of faith in Jesus Christ, I should not grieve as those who have no hope. One day I will see Jesse again, standing whole and perfect, living in the presence of God.

I thank God every day of my life that, because His Son died on Calvary, my son will live for eternity in His holy presence. At an early age, Jesse asked Jesus Christ to come into his life, forgive him of his sins, and to be the Lord and Savior of his life. Jesse was not perfect, but he was forgiven and washed in the blood of Jesus Christ.

Life happens. Graves come in all sizes. We are not promised another breath. What I am talking about is not religion. It is about a personal relationship with Jesus Christ. It is only through His blood that we are saved. There is no other way, no other plan. Until Jesus Christ returns to take His children home we are all going to face death. We are all going to spend eternity somewhere, either in heaven or hell. So what if today was your last day? Where would you spend your eternity?

CHILD OF THE KING

By LaVeta Boben

Where do I start? Well, I might as well start from the beginning.

My mom was abandoned by her mother at six months old and at sixteen years old she became a mother herself.

When I was young, I lived off and on with my paternal grandparents. I later learned that my grandparents would get phone calls that I was asleep in the car in a bar parking lot. I remember being taken to bars as a young child. I remember living on a creek bank with my mom when I was younger than five years old.

My father was never part of my life but his family was a huge part. We lived away from the majority of my mother's family. My mother did many things. She went to welding school; then she got her commercial driver's license. I remember living with my mom some, but I don't remember much until I reached third grade.

During that memory blackout I know I lived with my grandparents. I was a mawmaw's girl. My cousin's father had been killed when he was eighteen months old so he was living there too when his mom had to work. He has always said I was a mawmaw's girl because I got away with everything. But it was really because my grandfather molested me.

I vividly remember it. I remember praying that he wouldn't be the one that picked me up from my mom's when it was time to leave her.

When I was with my mom, I remember her having lots of different "friends." There were the ones who stayed with us, and the ones we stayed with. Mom stopped driving a truck when my sister was about six months old. That's when we lost our home and moved into my maternal grandfather's house in the country.

I remember going to the neighbors to eat because all there was to eat in the house was plain grits. We had nothing to go with them or in them. That's when my mom met my stepfather.

I went back to live with my grandparents. My mawmaw wouldn't let me see my mom anymore because she was living in a house with about fifteen other people and I would always come back with head lice.

8

I stayed with my grandparents for a while, probably a year or more, before my mom came and got me.

My stepfather was physically abusive. It didn't start, at least that I know of, until we all moved into our own house together. It was so incredibly bad and I didn't know what to do. Should I stay quiet or should I tell my mawmaw? But that would be mean having to live with my grandfather again.

I no longer had a safe place.

One very vivid night, I remember praying to God to make it stop. I could hear the screams and cries and I prayed harder. I didn't know whether to pray for us to leave or to stay. I just wanted us all to be safe. This went on for a few more years, then we moved to Minnesota. This took my grandparents out of the picture and I didn't see my grandfather again until he died.

But the fighting didn't stop; it just kept getting worse. On one of my mom's birthdays, the beating she got was so bad my stepfather thought he killed her. I thought for sure it was done then, but he just left jail and came home and on we lived.

There was a local church that had a van service and I loved going to the church. My sister and I would always go together.

At eleven years old, I asked God to come into my heart. I had been praying to God all my life. My aunt had taken me to church when I was little and I knew about Him, I just didn't know Him personally. Then, at eleven years old, I knew what it meant to have God, to know that regardless of everything I couldn't control God would always be there for me.

Things changed when Child Protective Services showed up at my school on the first day of sixth grade. There were a few days and then my stepfather was gone. My mom, sister, and I were good for a while. But it was hard. Mom worked and went to school and I had to take care of my sister.

My mom went back to having lots of "friends." One of them owned a resort and I started working there. I was fourteen years old and when school was out for the summer, I went there to stay and work until it was time for school to start back.

I did everything I thought was expected of me, a fourteen-year-old girl that was allowed to basically live on her own.

I got boys' attention the same way that I had seen my mom do my whole life. I drank, partied, and did drugs. Nothing was too much. I was having a great time. Until one day my mom and stepfather showed up to get me.

Yep, while I was gone, he came back.

And things went back to the way they were before. Back to our food stamps being sold for the little money they were worth to buy him drugs. But we all wanted him to have the drugs because it would get bad if he didn't have them. We went back to the water and the power being shut off. I looked forward to the winter because during cold, snowy winters in the north, companies wouldn't shut off anything because it was too dangerous.

This is about when I started doing the family grocery shopping. I would get the lady I babysat for to take me with her to the store when she went and I would shop for our family so I knew we would have food. This was my normal.

One day I was washing dishes and my stepfather hit me. I don't remember what exactly was said to set him off. He and my mom weren't fighting. I didn't get in the way. I just said something smart and he hit me. Not a little slap, but a full on punch.

I retreated into my room, and my mom kicked him out. She then told me that she believed me this time because she "saw it this time." Her comment crushed my whole world. She never believed any of the other things I told her about; she only believed what she saw. I carried that with me until after my mother's death.

I was seventeen when I moved out. It was a huge blow up. I came home from school and there were boxes in my room so I used them to pack and move out. I still don't know what they were doing in my room but I was done. I will never forget my sister crying in our mom's bed, wondering who was going to take care of her. She doesn't remember much of her childhood, but she remembers that day.

The next few years went by. Me and my boyfriend, now my husband, moved to another state, where we lived for about a year. I got pregnant before I was eighteen years old. My mom and sister moved while we were gone. At eighteen years old and pregnant I wanted to be near my mom and things were not going very well for my boyfriend and me where we were living, so we moved.

About a year after we moved, my boyfriend wanted to start going to church. He was working with someone that was leading him to Christ. We tried to go to church, but when we tried to leave the house, the car would mess up, so we would turn around to head home and it would start running fine again. We would try to leave again and it would do the same thing. We tried to go to church three times before we gave up and stayed at home.

While I was walking our dog I noticed a church about a mile down from our house so we went there. We stayed there for years. At that church we were led to get married, and my husband, mother, and sister were saved.

The one true regret my husband and I have from that time is that we were too scared to tell our pastor that we weren't married, so we went to the justice of the peace and eloped.

This might be a good story if it ended here. We found God, we got fed the Word, and we became good parents. But it doesn't end here. We failed once again.

Eventually we decided to move back to Minnesota. There we fell back into the world. We sold almost everything we worked so hard to get. We did drugs, lots and lots of drugs. Our marriage almost didn't make it either. Then one night, I realized I was becoming someone I was so scared of being.

We had a toddler and a baby and I was turning into my mom. I was putting my desires before my children.

We soon left Minnesota and went back to where we knew we could be around our church family and friends. There we could be around people who would help point us in the right direction and away from the people and the places that knew us before.

I do not know why we have to go through the things that we do, but here is what I do know: Romans 5:1–5 says, "Therefore, since we have been justified through faith, we have peace with God through our Lord Jesus Christ, through whom we have gained access by faith into this grace in which we now stand. And we boast in the hope of the glory of God. Not only so, but we also rejoice in our sufferings, because we know that suffering produces perseverance; perseverance, character; and character, hope. And hope does not put us to shame, because God's love has been poured out into our hearts through the Holy Spirit, who has been given to us."

None of us would be who we are without our story. Our life is our story. I wouldn't be this person if I had led a different life.

It wasn't until after my mother was killed that I was able to truly let go of everything and forgive her. I forgave her for not being the mother that I wanted. She didn't have a mother, and she truly did the best that she knew how.

I didn't share my story for a long time. Not until a friend asked me to. When I was asked to share, he told me to pray about it and I knew immediately. I knew God wanted me to share my story, but that still doesn't make it any easier for me to do.

We worked so hard to build the life we have. We built this life with God's hands. He was and is the only way that we could overcome so very much.

I was scared and worried about how people would look at us once they knew our dark secrets, the secrets we tried to hide.

Looking from the outside, my husband and I appear to have a fairytale life. We are high school sweethearts who are happily married raising our children together.

Would the people that once looked up to me and respected me see me different once they found out about my past?

Still the Holy Spirit came to me and gave me the courage to do it and here it is.

My story has made me stronger. God's grace has made me whole. He took those broken pieces and in the Potter's hands made me. He made me to be the wife and parent that He intended me to be.

This is my story. This is a taste at what I have overcome. I could have easily kept falling into the ways of the world as just another statistic, but with God I became more.

In 2014, I graduated college. I was the first on either side of my family to get a degree.

I was strongly influenced by a policeman that came to our house the night we thought my stepfather had killed my mom. He gave me peace and hope that it would be okay; that I would be okay. Now I have a criminal justice/juvenile justice degree.

My dream job was to work with kids; however, I believe God put me with adults so that I could better deal with the strain of the job. My position is similar to that of a social worker for inmates, but because I have been there, growing up in a less-than-ideal situation and strung out on drugs, I can tell them that I know what it is like, but I also know what it is like to be a child of the King, and with His grace we can turn our struggle into a triumph.

HE WILL SHOW UP

By Alicia Brown

Romans 8:28 says, "And we know that in all things God works for the good of those who love Him, who have been called according to His purpose."

It was the fall of 2014. In the South that means football. Lots of football. We were on the way to watch Destiny, our daughter cheer at a football game. Although we were running a little late as usual, we decided to stop at Walmart to grab some cash and be on our way. As we were backing out of the parking space a lady in another car backed into us.

On top of bills piling up, my husband's health problems, and new directions in ministry, this was something else we now had to worry about. When it rains, it pours, I guess. I felt like if it wasn't one thing, it was another. Thankfully her insurance company agreed to pay for the damages, and a couple of weeks later the car was in the shop getting fixed.

Later my son Christian was up at 1:00 a.m. sick with a stomach virus. I didn't feel well that day myself, but I got up to help him. All of a sudden I felt really weird really fast. With all my strength I barely whispered my husband's name, "Mike."

I wasn't sure if I was having a heart attack or stroke or what it was. I was still conscious enough to know to sit down quickly. I just remember staring at the top of my shower curtain and I knew I was about to pass out. I have passed out cold three times in my life, but this felt different.

I slumped over into the hallway. When I regained consciousness I was having trouble catching my breath. Although my vision was blurry, I could see my husband praying over me. My husband didn't like that I was having trouble breathing so we headed to the emergency room.

As we were on our way I told my family how much I loved them because I was unsure about making it to the hospital forty-five minutes away. It was 1:30 a.m. and my husband had his flashers on and was in a hurry to get me to the hospital. Of course he was speeding. We came to a

13

red light that no one was at so he went on through it. By this time we were being followed by a police officer. Mike had his flashers on so he figured the officer was following us to the hospital. Honestly he wasn't stopping regardless of why he was following us.

We got to the hospital and my husband grabbed a wheelchair and wheeled me in and handed me over to Destiny. He was going to speak to the police officer. My husband spent an hour and a half speaking with the officer, and he eventually wrote us four tickets.

After asking the doctor three times to test me for the flu, he finally agreed. I tested positive for the flu. Still feeling very weak in my legs with no explanation, I went home.

No one explained what happened to me except my sister in Christ. She told me I had vasovagal syncope. I researched the disease and discovered that people can die from vasovagal syncope within seconds or minutes.

Did God raise the dead through my husband's prayer? I believe so. My extreme breathlessness, immediate urge to use the restroom, and extreme muscle weakness makes me wonder. We had court within days of my hospital scare. Before court my husband told me he was not going to pay for those tickets.

I went to God in prayer that morning, and I was honest before Him. I prayed, "God, we need favor today. You know my bank account and it's not there. But either way we will accept Your will." Later that day Mike texted me and said we had to pay for them and the total was $494.50.

I was a little heartbroken because I didn't get my way. I felt as if I got smacked. God reminded me of my prayer. I said, "Yes God, You are still good and if You never do another thing for me You have done more than enough already. You gave us Your Son Jesus."

Just like Romans 8:28 says, I still deep down believed God had something good up His sleeve. I stopped worrying and just kept trusting in His goodness.

An hour later, while my husband was in line to sign some more paperwork, the attorney came by and took $100 off of the total. We were down to $394.50.

Later that night a preacher called and asked Michael to speak the following Sunday. The next morning Mike was talking to God about his message for that Sunday and asked God how he could preach when he had so much unforgiveness in his heart for that police officer. God gave him the message for that Sunday and it just so happened to be on forgiveness.

A few minutes later the body shop called to let my husband know he didn't do all the worked he had planned on our car. The car looked great and there was money left over.

Can you guess how much? It was $394.50. God provided right down to the penny.

From beginning to end, God had witnessed the whole entire thing. He was there the whole time. He said He would never leave us nor forsake us. God's ways are not our ways, and our faith is not by sight. If you're a child of God, hold on. He will show up. Keep believing. Keep serving. Keep obeying.

MY GREAT DEPRESSION, MY GREATER GOD

By Greg Brown

February 18, 2001. To a fan of stock car racing this date will live in infamy. It was on this particular Sunday that seven-time NASCAR champion Dale Earnhardt lost his life in a turn-four crash on the last lap of the Daytona 500.

Less than seven months later the World Trade Center's Twin Towers would be a heap of rubble. And at some point in the days between these two tragic events, my life too would hit a wall and tumble down all around me.

For the record, let me state that I am a NASCAR fan (though not as gung-ho as I once was) and I was, in fact, a huge fan of the Intimidator's black #3 Chevy.

Also, like most Americans, I remember with the utmost clarity where I was when the Twin Towers fell, when the Pentagon was attacked, and when United Flight 93 went down in a field in Pennsylvania. These are things people know. Things they won't ever forget. However, what I learned during this particular season in my life was there are some things that can't be known, especially concerning, for the lack of a more descriptive term, a demon by the name of depression.

During my 2001 struggle with this condition, illness, or whichever of the many categories into which it has been pigeonholed, I discovered that depression plays no favorites, attacks without warning and with extreme prejudice, and shows no mercy.

There were at the time circumstances in my life that made things difficult and stressful. No more so than usual, however. Yet still today, seventeen years removed from the most taxing elements of the situation, I find little, if any, correlation between the simple, everyday trials of life, and the emotional, physical, and spiritual anguish that overwhelmed me.

There's still so much I'll never know about depression, so much no one will ever know about it. But what little I do know I am sure of.

There was no warning, no signs, no earth-shattering event. I simply went to bed one night, woke up the next morning, and the moment my feet touched the carpet a tidal wave of weariness, fear, doubt, paranoia, self-hatred, and shame in one plunging crash all but destroyed me. Little did I know that the coming weeks would produce waves even more powerful and destructive, and that relief, at least the quick kind, would be out of the question.

I would eventually be diagnosed with clinical depression, and prescribed medication that would aid in returning to my life some sense of normalcy. That diagnosis, however, would be a long time coming, at least longer than I would have liked.

In the meantime my days would consist of extended periods of unprompted, uncontrollable, and inconsolable tears. Sometimes a single unkind memory, such as a harsh word someone said to me years earlier, would burrow into my mind and dominate my thoughts for hours on end. It was as though I was trapped in an endless downward spiral.

Life as I had known it simply ceased to exist. Unable to sleep I walked the floor at night, often tracing my steps over and over for hours at a time. Food had no taste. I had zero appetite. I became a recluse not wanting, even refusing, to see anyone, including my two young sons. Only my wife was allowed into my sanctuary of misery and, even then, begrudgingly. She once asked me if I was suicidal. My answer? "No, I'm not, but I really don't care to live anymore." An inconsiderate reply to be sure, but at the time an honest one.

I must say that during the entire ordeal my wife, Anita, was as steady and as strong as any person I've ever known in such circumstances. She, as they say, took the bull by the horns at the very outset and did not turn loose until she was certain I was well on the mend. She ran interference for me, never making excuses but being forcefully honest when protecting me. She did the leg work, the research, and made numerous phone calls which would eventually get me to the places and people who could help me the most. But, more than anything, she prayed.

The most important thing I learned, maybe my greatest takeaway from this season in my life, is that in the midst of great chaos and confusion, amid the noise of spiritual warfare and the clamor and clang of deceptive and destructive thoughts, the prayers of the saints always find a way through.

Yes, Anita prayed, and so did others. They prayed for my well-being and for my healing. They prayed for peace in my life and for days without fear. They prayed that through my struggles I would be made stronger, more willing in my surrender to God; more eager to fix my eyes on Him and not look away. You see, God had placed a specific calling on my life, and for twenty years I had been running from that calling. I learned later that many people were interceding on my behalf, and some had, in fact, been doing so for years.

While all this praying for my return to good health and a normal life was going on there were those who prayed that I would get serious with God. Not that I was a non-believer, a heretic or an apostate. I believed God is real and He is always with us.

Yet someone who knew me better than perhaps I knew myself was praying for me to claim the purpose for which I was created. Somewhere out there were people who had spoken to God on my behalf and had done so through the long years of my rebellion. And what would be the end result? Well, "the prayer of a righteous person is powerful and effective" (James 5:16), right?

Some two months after my struggle had abated (not ended, mind you, but only abated), I entered into the United Methodist Church candidacy program where I began preparing to become a local pastor.

This preparation would eventually bring my family and myself to the small community of Ariton, Alabama, where I have served as pastor of Ariton United Methodist Church and Pleasant Ridge United Methodist Church for the past fourteen years.

I have also been a teacher at Ariton High School for thirteen years now. All this from someone who swore he'd never leave his hometown, who at one point said he'd never be a preacher. Someone who ran from God, who wasted so many years. All this from someone who still deals with depression on occasion, but who has learned that God is faithful and ever-present. And that in Him we have the victory. I know with certainty that He never gives up on us, especially during the difficult, chaotic, and confusing periods of life.

"So," you might ask, "what about the depression? How exactly does it fit into this story? I mean, really, why bring it up when it was really God's answer to the prayers of the people that set you on the right path? It was Him calling you home."

In response to this I simply quote Romans 8:28, "And we know that in all things God works for the good of those who love Him, who have been called according to His purpose."

Did God cause my depression? Absolutely not. Did He allow it to happen? I believe He did. In hindsight, I see my struggle as a time of reckoning, a time when God did what He needed to do to get my undivided attention. He allowed me to reach a point where I could no longer run and no longer hide. A place where I had no choice but to finally make a choice. If not for my battle with depression I may never have made a choice at all. Praise Him in the valley? Yes sir, Praise Him in the valley.

Because of God's mercy and grace I have crashed into the walls of deception and fear and lived to tell about it. I continue to rise from the rubble of doubt, self-loathing, and shame. He can bring you, too, out of whatever pit you may find yourself spiraling into.

God is often referred to as the "hound of heaven." He pursues us relentlessly, longing for us to surrender to His great love, grace, and mercy. Would I have gone through my war with depression had I not ran from God's calling to preach? Who's to say? Yet through my twisting and turning inside that vortex of affliction, I began to see God as I'd never seen Him before, and I experienced the power of prayer in a refreshing and genuine way. God does indeed work all things together for good. Today, I am a pastor, a teacher, a husband, a father, and a grandfather. I am also a survivor of depression. More than anything I am a child of the most high God. I praise God that He never stopped chasing me.

GOD HAD A PLAN

By Dan Capps

In August 1962, I had a physical that was required for me to play football at Abbeville High School in Alabama. But Dr. McDavid found a heart murmur and my football career was put on hold until my senior year.

In 1963, I had my first heart catheterization and it was determined I had IHSS (Idiopathic Hypertrophic Sub-Aortic Stenosis), a thickening of the heart muscle mainly in the septum. Today, it is more commonly known as cardiomyopathy.

I inherited this disorder from my dad and probably my granddaddy. The doctors at the University of Alabama at Birmingham (UAB) hospital recommended no hard physical contact or exertion, but told me I could play baseball. Before my senior year, Daddy agreed to let me play football again, and I truly enjoyed it.

In June 1966, Fellowship Baptist Church was having its yearly revival, and to impress my girlfriend, I walked down to the front during the invitation. Shortly after that I was dunked under water — but not what I would consider truly, biblically baptized — at Tolbert Baptist Church. For the next forty-one years, I knew when to stand, when to sit, when to sing, and when to bow my head in any church I attended. I, without a doubt, was the best fake Christian in the entire world. But God knew the truth and knew how hard headed I was. God had a plan.

When I played both baseball and football, the win was never out of reach. Even if we were behind ten runs or four touchdowns. There is always hope. My cup is always half full, never half empty.

On December 20, 1985, God allowed me to marry the love of my life. Stephanie was and always will be the finest example of a Christian lady you will ever find. God had a plan.

In March 1987, I had experimental surgery for the IHSS that was supposed to help for four or five years but lasted twenty. God knew He needed more time because of my hardheadedness. Dr. Pacifico was the surgeon and on the cardiology team was a young doctor, Dr. Robert Bourge. God had a plan.

In January 2007, I had a defibrillator and pacemaker put in. There were supposed to be three wires going to my heart, but one detached itself so only two were in place. But, God only needed two.

On July 11, 2007, on a Wednesday night while Stephanie and the children were at Vacation Bible School, Huey Jones, who had worked for me as a teenager, came by the house and we were talking about fishing. Huey was, and still is, a member of the Abbeville Rescue Squad. He was about to leave when the defibrillator fired. He immediately called for an ambulance, and over the next three hours the defibrillator fired ninety times. God had a plan.

On July 19, 2007, after several very trying days at Southeast Alabama Medical Center and after several more firings of the defibrillator, Stephanie realized I was dying. She asked me if I died that night, did I know if I would go to heaven?

Crying, I truthfully told her, "No."

Stephanie prayed for me. We called our oldest child Alan, who is a pastor, and he arranged a teleconference with us and all our children. I asked God to forgive me of all my sins and to be the Savior of my life.

Two weeks later, Alan baptized me during the morning worship service at Pleasant Grove Baptist Church. For the next two months I fought congestive heart failure. Fluid was being drawn from my lungs several times a week. Out of desperation, the pulmonary specialist suggested I consider being evaluated for a heart transplant. It was then he revealed the size of my heart by showing me an X-ray. My heart covered the middle of my chest.

Back in June 1958, my mother had opened the Tastee Freeze in Abbeville and ran it for more than forty-four years. During this time, all the young people in Abbeville hung out at the Tastee Freeze. God had a plan.

One of those young people was Kirby Bland, who in 2007 was the Chief of Surgery at UAB. Stephanie contacted an Abbeville High School classmate of Dr. Bland's to see if we could be seen by some of the UAB doctors.

Dr. Bland's good friend at UAB was Dr. Kay, a rhythm specialist, and my rhythm was the problem I was having, or so we thought.

A few days later we saw Dr. Kay, who told us I did not need an ablation, and he recommended I be evaluated for a heart transplant. The head of the UAB heart transplant unit was Dr. Robert Bourge. The same Dr. Robert Bourge who was on my cardiology surgery team back in 1987. God had a plan.

I was given every test known to man and a few I think they just made up. The last doctor I saw was the head of psychiatry, and when he walked in he asked me what was the first thing I wanted to do if I had a heart transplant? I looked at Stephanie, smiled, and said, "Find a bream bed and have at it!" He knew nothing about fishing in the South and left the room very quickly. All he heard was "bed" and "have at it." I just wanted to go fishing with my wife!

I made the transplant list and more testing followed. Twelve days later, on October 1, 2007 around 1 p.m., while we had some visitors from Abbeville High School, we were told there might be a heart available and we would know by 4 p.m.

Normally there is a selection process where several transplant candidates would be evaluated for an available heart, but not in this case. I was the only patient prepped for the heart. God had a plan.

At 7 p.m. I was taken down and parked outside of the operating room. In an hour, a tech came and turned off the defibrillator. When the operating room doors opened, I knew God was with me because that was the whitest and most beautiful room I had ever seen.

About 2 a.m., Dr. Kirklin — who is the son of Dr. Kirklin, Sr. who started the UAB heart research in the mid 1960s that led to the first heart transplant in 1981 — met with Stephanie and the children and discussed what he had done. My old heart was very, very big and was not really beating but just shaking like a big bowl of jello. He said it would be touch and go for a while. But, God had a plan.

After I was moved from CICU, I returned to the same room I had been in before the transplant and we were told that was very unusual. One nurse who had rotated off for three days thought I was still on the waiting list. When he returned to work he could not believe I had received a new heart. We were there because God had a plan.

After a transplant, the family is both emotionally and physically drained, and our room was directly across from the nurses' station which made it very easy for the nurses to care for me.

Two weeks later, we left UAB and moved into The Townhouse which is part of the UAB system. We made trips back to UAB every few days for tests, catheterizations, etc. During this time my medications were constantly monitored and adjusted. The trips back to UAB were reminders of how blessed and fortunate we were.

We came home six weeks after the transplant, which was just before Thanksgiving, and were welcomed by our whole family. Needless to say we had a great Thanksgiving in 2007.

Six months after the transplant I returned to work at the alternative school in Abbeville. Six months and eight days after the transplant I called a high school baseball game. Baseball was the carrot dangled in front of me I used as motivation.

God still has a plan. I currently take the least amount of anti-rejection medication of any UAB heart transplant patient, and I have no restrictions on my activities or my diet. We return to UAB twice a year: in March for a general check-up and in October for my yearly catheterization.

I give God and my organ donor the credit for saving my life. I will always be thankful to God and the person that gave me the gift of life. Without the gift from my donor, my story would be quite different. If it had not been for my heart transplant, I would not be alive today. My donor turned loss into hope. I want to make sure I make my life count. I do not want my donor's gift to be wasted. My life is filled with new appreciations and priorities.

There are two Bible verses on the cards I give people when the occasion arises: Ezekiel 36:26 says, "I will give you a new heart and put a new spirit in you; I will remove from you your heart of stone and give you a heart of flesh."

God did this in the Southeast Alabama Medical Center when for the first time in my life I was saved. The other verse is Jeremiah 29:11, which says, "'For I know the plans I have for you,' declares the Lord, 'Plans to prosper you and not harm you, plans to give you hope and a future.'"

My future? Daily I try to be a Christian example. I want others to realize what God can do for them regardless of where they have been or what they have done.

NO GIVING UP

By Sandra Cruikshank

The day started as a normal work day. But after a visit to the doctor and confirmation that I was pregnant, it became the most exciting day of my life.

Everyone in our immediate family was very happy. My husband Tom's grandmother said from the beginning it would be a boy and we had to continue the family name of Thomas Chandler Cruikshank.

Tom's grandmother was right. Our son was born and we named him Thomas Chandler III. In the line of Thomas Chandlers, he was the sixth. Chuck, which was the nickname we gave him, was born at Lyster Army Hospital in Fort Rucker, Alabama. He was six weeks premature and weighed four and a half pounds.

That day changed our lives in a way we never saw coming and it was the first of many times we would ask, "Why God?"

Chuck was immediately placed in an incubator and we could not hold him. On the third day Chuck began to run high fevers and the pediatrician told us that because he was premature and now running high fevers he wanted him to be airlifted to Kessler Air Force Base Medical Center in Biloxi, Mississippi.

The hospital at Kessler was a major pediatric medical center for the military. They immediately began to run tests on him, and within a couple of days he was diagnosed with a rare form of meningitis called E. coli Meningitis, a very lethal form of the infection.

They cultured his brain fluid to determine what medication would work, and the only medication that would work against the meningitis was gentamicin. Because of the side effects — deafness and or blindness — we had to sign a consent form for the medication to be used.

Chuck spent the first four months of his life at Kessler Medical Center. He had good days and bad days and on some of his worst days he was packed in ice because his fever would get up to 107 or 108 degrees.

Many times we held vigil by his bedside because he was not expected to live. Chuck had severe brain damage due to the meningitis and extremely high fevers.

He did survive, but he developed hydrocephalus and had to have bilateral shunts to keep the fluid from collecting in his brain. That surgery was the first of dozens to revise the shunts so they would work properly. It always included a trip back to Kessler from Fort Rucker and days in the hospital.

He continued to have revisions until he was around ten years old when his head finally stabilized, and it was determined that the shunts were no longer needed but would be left in just in case.

Chuck had seizures because of the hydrocephalus. Chuck's head grew way out of proportion to his body, and because of that he could not stand or sit without support. Chuck's left hip and leg was the next problem we dealt with.

Chuck had no hip socket so numerous surgeries were done to get scar tissue to form a socket around the head of his hip. He was in a body cast three different times but the deformity was so severe we decided to stop the surgeries knowing Chuck would never walk.

Early on we could carry him, but as he began to grow we had a special stroller he could ride in, and he eventually got a wheelchair. To say that Chuck was a trooper through all of this is an understatement.

Chuck did lose his hearing but could see. He could not talk but learned sign language early on. The brain damage from the meningitis left him without use of his arms or hands and totally dependent on others for his care. Thankfully neither the hydrocephalus nor meningitis reoccurred. However, Chuck did have to have bowel resection surgery plus a super pubic catheter and a colostomy.

On one of our many visits back to Kessler we had a doctor tell us that Chuck needed to be put into an institution because he probably would not live to be a teenager.

Chuck is now forty-six years old.

Chuck's life has been filled with many doctor visits, surgeries, and hospital stays. We have sat many hours by his bedside in hospitals. He is totally unable to care for himself. He is deaf, mute, and confined to a wheelchair.

We have been blessed that Chuck has been able to attend schools for people with special needs. These types of schools are a Godsend to people like Chuck and their families. All the teachers and aides are trained to work with all types of special needs and are God's angels here on earth. Chuck goes to Vivian B. Adams School in Ozark, Alabama every day. A bus picks him up at home and delivers him back in the afternoon. I would say it is one of the best facilities for people with special needs that we have ever been associated with.

Tom and I both have been asked many times how we have managed without giving up. Why didn't we put Chuck in an institution? One thing Tom and I determined early on was that we would care for Chuck at home as long as God gave us the strength to do so. I can say without hesitation that it has not been an easy task, but it has been a lifelong learning experience for our family.

As we look back we always see the hand of God at work in our lives and in Chuck's life. It amazes me the people God has placed in our lives to guide us through this. While we have had to learn to live and care for a person with special needs, Chuck is the joy of our lives. There are very few days that he doesn't smile. His smile is infectious. He draws people in with his smile. He is truly a joy to all who come in contact with him.

One day I got an email from a friend titled the "Black Dot." It was the story of a professor who gave his class a pop quiz. He gave each student a piece of paper with a black dot in the center of the page and asked them to write about what they saw. Needless to say the students were surprised and confused.

When he took up the papers and looked at them, all of the students had written about the black dot. No one had written anything about the white part of the paper.

This is what happens in our life when we focus on the black dot. Yes, we could have taken the doctor's advice early on and put Chuck in a facility for people with special needs, but God gave Chuck to us and I strongly believe that Chuck would not be living today if we had done that. He was a special gift, and we are challenged on a daily basis to care for the needs that Chuck has. We could have looked at it as a black dot. We could have completely forgotten about the white piece of paper. The white piece of paper is what God wants us to look at. He wants us to see that life is His gift to us. He wants us to love and care for and celebrate Chuck.

We could focus on the black dot — the health issues that Chuck has and will continue to have, the fact that we have to care for his every need. But Chuck is so much more than that. Chuck reaches out to people, and if you watch Chuck closely, you can see that he communicates with his eyes.

We have learned many lessons through this. First and foremost, we learned that God will never give us more than we can handle through Him. He is ever present with us. Some nights I will wake up and hear Chuck laughing and babbling and I tell people that he and God are having a good time together.

Yes, there are days that I am burdened and disheartened, but I remember the verse in Matthew 11, "Take my yoke ... and find rest for your souls. My yoke is easy and my burden is light."

Psalm 46:10 says, "Be still and know that I am God." I can sit and be still and silent and suddenly the burden is gone.

Instead of walking around tired and heavy-hearted I can be lighthearted knowing that nothing that I do is being done alone; God is right by my side. He is waiting patiently to give me rest and peace.

Lamentations 3:21–22 says, "Yet this I call to mind and therefore I have hope: Because of the Lord's great love we are not consumed, for His compassions never fail." God's compassion never ends. He is always willing to respond knowing what our every need is. So instead of looking at the black dots in our lives, try to look at the white part of the paper because that is where we'll find God's blessings and love.

When we lived in Florida, we had a pastor, Brother Jack, and he and Chuck were great buddies. In one of his sermons he said he had a dream that he was in the pulpit one Sunday morning and the back doors flew open and Chuck was running down the aisle shouting "Brother Jack! Brother Jack!"

One day God will call Chuck to his forever home. His body will be new, and he will be running and talking and smiling. It will probably take him a thousand years to say everything that is bottled up inside of him.

Until that day comes we will continue to love and care for Chuck with the help of God, our family, and the multitude of friends that He has placed in our lives.

YOU ARE NOT ALONE

By Boyd Deal

My daddy came from a large family. There were six children — four boys and two girls. They lived on the same farm that I grew up on. Daddy bought the farm from his brothers and sisters so he could raise our family there. The people that grew up on farms during this time normally had large families so the kids could help work on the farm. My family was no different. I was one of five children — four boys and one girl.

He always had a lot of family members, employees, and friends around the house. They would sit around telling stories and laughing. Daddy loved people, telling stories, and laughing. I can still remember his laugh.

Daddy was very intelligent even though he dropped out of school after the ninth grade. Many people have shared stories with me about his mathematical skills. They tell me that he could figure up the price of a house faster in his head than most could with a calculator. He was obviously pretty gifted with these skills since he ran a successful farming operation and two separate construction companies. One of the companies built homes and the other built chicken houses.

Daddy worked hard, and he worked us like young men from the time I was old enough to remember it. I remember him dropping us off at a new home he was building when I was six or seven years old and my brothers and I worked all day installing insulation in the attic of the house. My oldest brother would have only been eleven or twelve years old and he was supervising the project for us.

We built chicken houses on the family farm when I was six years old. The chicken houses were full of chickens that laid eggs. I don't know if you have ever had any experience with layer houses, but I can assure you they are a lot of work. We would get off the school bus every afternoon after school, grab a snack, and then go straight to the chicken houses. After we finished picking up eggs, they all had to be cleaned, graded, and stored in the cooler.

The chickens laid eggs seven days a week. Weekends and holidays meant nothing to those chickens. I hated those chickens and picking up those eggs. In fact, I disliked picking up eggs so much that I never picked up Easter eggs at school or church since we had several thousand to pick up every day. Who would want to hunt a few eggs at school or church when that was what you did every day?

Daddy was forty-four years old and I was ten years old when we found out that he had cancer. Once the doctors found the cancer, they told him he would be lucky if he lived six months. He died six days short of six months.

Cancer is a terrible disease. I recall watching his body waste away and change daily. The things I recall most involved weight loss, hair loss, his sickness from the medicine and treatments, and having to have help getting around in his wheelchair. Daddy was six foot, six inches tall, and he weighed about 190 pounds when he found out he had cancer. At the time he died he weighed less than 100 pounds.

Daddy was a proud man so I am sure these things bothered him though I do not recall him ever saying anything about them. These are the things I used to think about as a child and as a young man. However, now that I am a father myself, I can only imagine the things that he was suffering from that had nothing to do with the cancer. He suffered from a lot of physical things due to the cancer, but I bet those were not his biggest concerns.

Can you imagine how he felt knowing he was about to die and he was only forty-four years old? Can you imagine how he felt knowing that he was leaving behind a wife and five young kids? Can you imagine the thoughts that he had regarding the wellbeing of his kids? How would they all make it in life? What would happen to the family farm? What would happen to the businesses he started?

I cannot tell you anything about his thoughts or concerns. What I can tell you is that he handled each of these things much better than I would have done. I cannot remember seeing my daddy cry or get upset about the sickness and death he had to face.

I remember standing next to the casket at Daddy's funeral crying. Daddy was gone. I loved him, and I knew I was going to miss him. However, it was more than that. Even though I was only 10 years old, I knew life was about to change. Daddy had been our provider, but now he was gone. Daddy had been our protector, but now he was gone. I could not help but wonder what would happen to me, my brothers, and my sister.

Losing Daddy changed a lot of things around our house. He has been gone for more than forty-five years. He has missed a lot. So have I.

I never had a chance to talk with him about girls, buying a house or a car. I never had a daddy that could take up for me when I was being mistreated. I didn't have a daddy that could teach me how to hunt, fish, or play ball, or attend my events at school.

Losing Daddy made us grow up and forced us to have to do things that kids should never have to do. I recall being about twelve years old, and we had a dog that had been in the family for several years. The dog got in the chicken houses and killed a couple hundred chickens. Mother said that someone had to shoot him. No one wanted do it. I finally told mother that I thought I could take care of it. I took him behind the chicken houses next to a big beautiful oak tree. I picked the spot next to the oak tree since that is where he would be buried. I called him up to me and then I shot him.

I can still recall that event in my mind. I cried as I was walking from the house to the wooded area, and I continued to cry until after we got him buried. As a twelve-year-old kid you are never mentally prepared to handle that kind of responsibility. This was not something that I enjoyed. I just knew that mother was depending on one of us to do it since we could not afford for our dog to get back in the chicken houses.

My brothers, sister, and I did not have a childhood like most kids. During the time in life when most kids are playing, watching cartoons, and enjoying life, our family was acting and working like adults. When I was in school, I used to hear people talk about watching their favorite TV shows, playing board games, or doing things with their family. I do not have any of those stories. We worked hard when Daddy was alive and that continued after he passed since we had to provide for our family.

We were able to keep the farm and work on it for about three or four years after Daddy died, but then mother decided to sell it. Even though we worked all the time growing up, it paid dividends for me. The work ethic I established as a child taught me some valuable lessons. While in college, I worked as many as three jobs at a time in order to pay my own way through college, and I finished in four years without any debt.

Losing my daddy when I was ten years old has been one of the worst things that has ever happened to me. However, God can take a bad situation and make the impossible possible. As bad as this loss was, I can now tell you that God used that terrible experience to bless me and Daddy.

If Daddy had not gotten cancer, he may never have been saved. Shortly before his death, Daddy asked God into his heart. I didn't realize it for a long time, but I can now tell you that Daddy's salvation was more important than for me to have him here with me.

Also, losing Daddy made me a better father. God used this terrible event in my life to mold me into the man that I am today. God used that void in my life to motivate me to be the best daddy I could be, and I refuse to stop trying to improve as long as God gives me breath to breathe.

It took me a long time, but I finally got to a point that I could praise God for His love and mercy even though Daddy passed away too young. God placed good, godly people in my life to help influence me. They motivated and encouraged me as I went through life. Many of these people believed in me when I did not believe in myself. I think they saw something in me that I could not see.

I know from experience what it feels like not to have a father. I have seen families where the father is missing in action. I have seen families where the father is not the spiritual leader and financial provider for his household. I have often heard people say that they did bad things, or they made bad decisions because their dad was not in their life. I have done the opposite. I have used it to motivate and strengthen me.

On March 22, 1991, something happened to me. From the moment Bradley was born my life changed and I will never be the same again. God has blessed me in so many ways, but no gift has been better than having my boys. I am so thankful that God allowed me to have this experience. Everything about being a daddy has made me want to be a better person.

I started a family journal shortly after Bradley was born and wrote in it until my second son Tyler finished high school. It took me twenty years to write the journal. I have to admit that losing Daddy was the thing that drove me to start and complete this labor of love. It contains 515 pages of memories that involve sporting events, hunting, fishing, camping, working around the house, vacations, growth charts, and many other things. However, the most important things in the journal are on pages 132, 135, and 137. Page 132 documents when Tyler accepted Christ and when he was baptized. Pages 135 and 137 documents when Bradley accepted Christ and when he was baptized.

These pages are a reminder that we will all get to spend eternity together in heaven. Trust me, there is no better feeling than that.

Bradley and Tyler will never know the amount of joy they have added to my life. I have given up things many people think are important so I could provide for my family. None of those things could even begin to add as much joy to my life as my family has provided for me. I have never once thought of them as a burden or that they were keeping me from getting things. They are my biggest blessings. I want my kids to know that they are more valuable to me than anything I own. All of my things will belong to someone else after I am gone, but hopefully the way I treated my family will affect the way they live and act. I hope my boys think of me as being compassionate, committed, giving, and loving. But most of all, I hope they remember me as a Christian that loved to serve God.

You will face a hardship or loss in your life. When you do, please remember that you are not alone. Your suffering will cause you to struggle, and that is normal. You will most likely want some answers as to why it happened. Unfortunately, most of the time, we never get the answers. God's ways are not our ways. All I can tell you that might give you some encouragement is that God used one of the worst things in my life to change my life for the better. I do not understand why I had to suffer without a daddy, but I am thankful for the way this suffering has changed and blessed my life.

THANK GOD FOR SECOND CHANCES

By Boyd Deal

It's hard to believe that it has been more than thirty years since I got divorced. It has been so long that most people do not even know I was previously married. Many of my friends and family were not even born when it happened. It is difficult to open up those old memories and expose my weaknesses. However, if my story can help just one person, then it will be worth the challenge.

I have no desire to list everything that contributed to my divorce, but I do think it is important to provide some information so hopefully people can learn from the mistakes both of us made. I do not want this story to create conflict. I have always been able to maintain a great relationship with all of my ex-wife's family, and I do not want to do anything to damage any of those relationships. Therefore, there is no need to get deep into the weeds about all the things that led to my divorce. I could point out all of the mistakes that my ex-wife made and she could point out all of mine, but the final result would not change.

On October 12, 1985, I married the girl that I had dated throughout high school and college. She had been involved in nine years of my life. To this day, when I think back to the events that occurred during high school and college, she is in almost every memory.

We started liking each other before we were old enough to date. I was in the ninth grade and she was in the tenth grade. The difference in our grade level during high school was not much of a problem; however, it did create some challenges when she went to college. She was involved in her events at college and I had a very busy schedule with sports and the normal activities that occur during a senior year of high school. We broke up for a few months, but eventually we were able to work out those differences and we started dating again.

Prior to getting married, our relationship continued to have some struggles. We worked through some challenges before so we thought we could overcome the challenges that we would face as a married couple. However, that was not the case.

We separated on the weekend of our second anniversary and we divorced in March 1988.

How could anyone get a divorce? Be careful thinking that. My struggle may look different than yours, but it was real. I never wanted to carry that label, but it happened. Divorce is a difficult thing. Some people reading this cannot understand the pain it involves, and some know firsthand the way it can break your heart.

Sometimes we can plan for the events in our life, but those plans can change quickly if both people do not stay focused on what is really important. Those things are God, love, and commitment.

We struggled finding a church that we enjoyed attending together. I wanted to attend one church and she wanted to attend another. At the end of our marriage, the preacher at her church caused some of our biggest problems. He told my ex-wife that marriage was about being happy, and if she was not happy then she should leave. I believe marriage is about more than just being happy; it is about commitment.

Unfortunately, he never said anything about the commitment a couple makes when they get married. He never said anything about the biblical guidelines regarding marriage and divorce. Most marriages will encounter stress and hardship. If you marry someone just so your spouse can make you happy then you probably married for the wrong reason.

I was faithful to my ex-wife, but I made some mistakes. I regret not being the husband I should have been in my first marriage. I should have spent more time with her. I should have been the spiritual leader of our house. I failed at these things.

I have asked God to forgive me for anything I may have done to contribute to our divorce. I believe with all of my heart that God has done that.

We stayed together for two years, and she moved out on the weekend of our second anniversary. It was planned that way. Our goal was to stay together until our second anniversary so we could say that we made it two years. You may think that sounds silly, but we were young and in the back of my mind I was hoping we might find something that was worth fighting for. Unfortunately, in the end you cannot be the only one willing to fight to save the relationship.

There are days in your life that you will never forget. The day my ex-wife moved out is one of those days. I left home for the day so it would be easier on each of us and she moved out while I was gone.

When I arrived back at the house that night, I felt a pain I had never felt before. It was the lowest point of my life. We had planned for the separation, but I was not mentally prepared for it. A home that had once been full of love and laughter was now half empty, quiet, and lonely.

I had felt the pain of failure before but nothing that compared to this pain. I was embarrassed. I thought everyone was judging me. I could not help but be consumed by what I thought everyone else was thinking and saying.

I felt numb for several months. I never thought that I was in any type of depression. However, I discovered that there were times when the walls at my house were closing in on me. I soon learned I had to get out more and be around my family and friends if I was going to overcome this season in my life.

Several family members and friends spent time with me and helped me during that dark season of my life. Two of those people were my sister and a co-worker. They were my biggest supporters during my darkest days. My sister called me all the time and included me on her family vacations with her in-laws. Jackie Davis, a co-worker, always knew when I was having a bad day. I can recall her coming into my office and sitting down just to make sure I was okay. Her friendship has been priceless in my life. We are not related by blood and she is not listed in my family tree, but she is part of my family.

I remember praying and asking God to help me overcome this struggle that I was going through and to take my pain away. He taught me that I had to learn to love myself again before I could love someone else again. A friend of mine calls it "top-down happiness." I had to get my mind right before I could let other people close to me and before other people could enjoy being around me.

I dated a lot of girls but I always had a wall up to keep from being hurt again. For two years, I wouldn't go on more than three dates with anyone. I knew that rule would keep me from getting close to someone. I did not want to feel the pain of another broken relationship.

A close friend asked me once if I thought I would ever remarry. I told her that I wanted to but I was not sure God was going to put another person in my life. I did not realize it at the time, but God was repairing my broken heart. He knew I needed to be healed before I could get married again. It had to be in God's timing, not mine.

Sometimes you find love when you are not even looking for it. Sometimes you find love when you don't think it's even possible. That is what happened to me.

My sister tried to get me to ask out Leah, now my wife, for two years. I did not want to since she was five years younger than me and still in college. Finally, I agreed to ask her out so my sister would stop bugging me about it. After the first date with Leah I knew she was a special person. After our third date I knew I loved her, and I knew she was the one I wanted to marry. Prior to meeting Leah, I never thought it was possible to fall in love with someone that fast. I think the way it turned out is ironic because of the three date rule that I implemented for the previous two years. I think that was God's way of showing me He has a sense of humor. God knew what I needed before I knew it myself.

Some people will tell you not to rush into marriage, and I would agree that is probably the best advice in most cases. But I need to remind you that I dated my ex-wife for nine years and we were only married for two years. I dated Leah for five months, and we have been married since 1990. I can promise you it is not about the number of dates you had with a person; it is about both people being committed to making the marriage work.

I cannot begin to tell you how thankful I am that God put Leah in my life. She has been my biggest encourager. She believes in me. She trusts me. She made me want to be a better person. Leah has always been committed to our marriage, and she continued to love me even when we did not agree on things. But most importantly, she was the one that got me back involved in church. There is no doubt that putting God first in our life is the thing that has blessed our marriage more than anything else.

During my darkest days I sometimes had difficulty feeling God's presence. However, I now know that He was with me every step. Joshua 1:9 says, "Have I not commanded you? Be strong and courageous. Do not be afraid; do not be discouraged, for the Lord your God will be with you wherever you go."

It was only through His love, mercy, and forgiveness that I was able to overcome my broken heart. If you feel brokenhearted, I hope you will find happiness soon. I believe the best medicine for happiness involves putting God first in your life and surrounding yourself with family and friends.

There are events that completely change the course of our lives. Graduating high school, graduating college, choosing a career, getting married, and having kids are a few of those things. My divorce did the same thing in my life. I could have allowed my previous marriage and the divorce to define my future relationships in life, but I did not. My divorce could have made me bitter. I think I used it to make me better. This failure has helped make me a better husband and father. I believe my past weaknesses are now some of my biggest strengths.

I think the most valuable lesson from my story is the way God has blessed me after my divorce. Even though I felt broken He never gave up on me. He placed Leah and both of my boys in my life. All three of them have allowed me to experience a love greater than I thought was possible. He has allowed me to serve Him in more ways than I deserve.

God has blessed me more than I ever asked Him to do and I will always praise Him for His blessings.

God is always doing more than we can see.

WHY ME, LORD?

By Leah Deal

My childhood was like most every other kid's in our town. I played hard and enjoyed all kind of games and activities. Our family spent a lot of time together and I loved it. We played games and participated in sporting events with each other.

Many of you that are reading this have experienced difficulty and pain. I have had my share too. I have had nine surgeries and four of them have been to correct problems related to my back and neck.

When I was twelve years old, I started experiencing my first back problems. For almost forty years now, my back pain has been my biggest challenge. For many years I have wondered, *Why me, Lord.*

I have four siblings and I am the one that has had to endure so many medical problems. In my younger years it never really bothered me. I just dealt with it and kept going. The older I got the more I wondered why God allowed me to go through so much.

When I was twelve years old, they discovered that I had scoliosis.

Scoliosis is an abnormal curvature of the spine. Some of the problems related to scoliosis are tingling or numbness in the legs, permanent deformities, breathing problems, and heart problems. Based on my condition, my doctor recommended surgery to help prevent my problems from getting worse. The surgery went as expected, but I had some complications with my recovery. The recovery in the hospital was expected to take one week, but because of the complications, I had to spend a month in the hospital.

Recovering from my Scoliosis surgery was a long journey. It did not take long for me to discover that I was not able to do some of the things I was once able to do. Over time, however, God blessed me by allowing me to participate in many activities. I played basketball, softball, cheered, and ran track at my high school. He even blessed me to be able to continue my basketball career at the community college I attended. I loved playing basketball, and I have always been grateful that I had the opportunity to play it in college.

Fast forward to October 3, 1992. I faced a situation that has created some of my biggest challenges related to my back issues. That was the day I was involved in an automobile accident.

I was four months pregnant with our second child at the time of the accident. After this accident, my back problems caused me to endure a level of pain I had never experienced before. Since that time, I have had two surgeries on the lower part of my back and one surgery on my neck. My back pain has changed some of the goals I had in life, and it has prevented me from doing some of the things that I would have loved to been able to do with my kids.

My husband and I wanted four kids, but we decided to stop after our second child was born since I had to be confined to bed rest for the last two months of my pregnancy.

I would have loved to have been able to play basketball, ride a sea doo or boat, and travel on long road trips with my husband and boys, but I have not been able to do those things. Most of the time, I was not even able to play games with them on the floor at our house. I would have enjoyed the canoe trips and games that our church groups participated in, but I was unable to do those things, too.

Reading the Bible and studying God's Word has brought me a lot of comfort during the most difficult times in my life. The Bible provides encouragement for me by the way people handle their pain and suffering and the way God provided many miracles.

The Bible shows me how other believers suffered but continued to praise and serve during their hardships. Paul, Job, and Jesus all encountered pain and suffering in their life, but they remained faithful. The purpose of Paul's thorn in the flesh was so he would not boast about the things he was able to do. The purpose of Job's suffering was to show his loyalty, love, and faithfulness to God. The purpose of Jesus's suffering was for us to have eternal life. I would never compare my pain and suffering to what they went through, but I know if they suffered greatly and still remained faithful then I can do the same thing. Unfortunately, I do not understand or know the purpose of my suffering, but God does. Hopefully, one day He will reveal that to me. However, even if He does not, I will continue to worship and serve Him.

God's Word also shows me how He provided many miracles throughout the Bible, and that allows me to understand He is in control of all circumstances. Nothing is impossible for God. His Word reveals that time and time again. He created the universe. He saved Daniel in the lion's den. He allowed Abraham and Sarah to conceive a child at an old age. He protected and saved Shadrach, Meshach, and Abednego in the fiery furnace. He gave David the ability to face and kill a giant. He parted the Red Sea. He made the blind to see. He raised Jesus from the dead. Each of these miracles proves that God can take away my pain and heal me if He chooses. However, even if He does not do it, I will continue to praise Him and love Him.

With the help of God, my family, my friends, and my coworkers, I have been successful at reaching several milestones and some big goals. My retirement was one of those goals. May 26, 2017, was my final day as a full-time teacher. Because of my back problems I always wondered if I would be able to teach long enough to retire or if I would end up having to go on disability. Even though it was a difficult journey, I was able to make it to retirement. I am very grateful God allowed me to accomplish that goal.

Even though I have experienced a lot of medical problems, I acknowledge that God has blessed me in so many ways. My husband Boyd and our two sons, Bradley and Tyler are three of my biggest blessings.

First, God blessed me with a husband that has stood by me in these difficult times and taken care of mine and the boys' needs. He did whatever it took for life to go on. He has lived the part of our vows "in sickness and in health." I know the difficult times were hard on him because he had to do so many things.

Second, God blessed me with two wonderful boys. Sometimes they had a hard time understanding my medical problems, but eventually they learned what I could and couldn't do.

Finally, both of my parents are still alive and they are very involved in my life. I have one sister and three brothers that I love very much. We have shared countless memories together. As I look back on my life, it is easy to see that God used a lot of people to bless me. I will always be indebted to them, and I will never forget the love and support they have shown to me.

I have encountered seasons in my life that have been very difficult. At times the pain was extreme.

I stated earlier that for many years I wondered, "Why me, Lord." I now understand that this journey has allowed me to walk closer to God. During my pain and suffering is when I found myself praying to God all the time. It was during my difficult times that I found myself focusing on the pain when I first woke up in the morning, as I went throughout the day, and it was the last thing on my mind when I laid my head down at night. I was praying to God morning, day, and night.

It would be easy to get depressed if I only focused on my pain and suffering. However, when I look at all the ways God has blessed me, I realize that I have been given more than I deserve. I rejoice in the fact that I will spend eternity in heaven with God. I have experienced God's love, mercy, and forgiveness in my life, so I understand that my pain is temporary. One day all of my pain and suffering will be removed. One day my body will be healed and I will be able to walk the streets of gold in heaven and praise God forever and ever.

The most important part of my story is that I know God's Word, and I know how it ends. We win.

UNCLAIMED TREASURE … UNEXPECTED ENDING

By Kim Earwood

More than thirty years ago, I worked at an electric co-op during summer and Christmas breaks, and then again for a while after I finished graduate school.

There was a wonderful lady who worked with me named Martha. Each day it was a blessing to work with her and always offered an adventure. One day she and I embarked on a conversation about marriage. I told her I didn't know if I would ever marry and I might be an old maid.

She said, "Oh no, you would never be an old maid, but an unclaimed treasure."

After all of these years that has stuck with me. At the time she shared that with me, I was dating someone who I later was engaged to but never married.

The remainder of my twenties and into my thirties, I dated lots of guys — more than I can count. It got to the point where dating was not just comical, but also exhausting.

I once asked a good friend and coworker if he knew someone who had invited me on a date.

My friend responded, "If you go out with that guy, I will never speak to you again". Needless to say, I did not go out with that particular suitor. I shared that same story with my sister, and it was then she deemed me "the jackass magnet."

After that, I came to the conclusion that if the good Lord wanted me to be with someone, then he would send them to me.

In July 2011, while visiting with my momma and daddy at their church, I met a man who would later become my husband. His name was Larry and he was a smooth talker.

He told my daddy, "Dale, you never told me you had such a beautiful daughter. Where have you been keeping her?"

Daddy responded, "Somebody has got to earn me a living." And we all laughed.

After that meeting, Larry pursued me for a couple of weeks, telling me that I needed to come home and let him take me out.

Finally, I gave in. From our first date on we had so much fun and really enjoyed our time together. Although we lived 150 miles from one another, we made it work.

We had a whirlwind romance. We dated for ten months and then married.

At forty-three years old, this "unclaimed treasure" had been claimed. I was so happy to find the love of my life, the person I would be with forever ... so it seemed.

The first eighteen months of marriage were no joke. There were so many things for both of us to get used to. We had to combine households, rent a storage unit and fill it with all kinds of stuff we owned and didn't need, and endure numerous health surprises. It affected both of us, but once all of it was worked out, we had a pretty good marriage and life together.

Then June 2017 came. Larry had some unexpected issues with his heart. Two of his arteries were almost completely blocked and he had to have stents put in.

We felt so fortunate that these problems were quickly discovered and corrected and that Larry had not suffered a heart attack. His cardiologist was actually amazed he was alive.

Unfortunately, about two months after Larry's heart procedure, life began to change, not only for Larry, but for both of us.

Larry's personality changed, and he became a different person. Some days I didn't know which version of Larry I was going to wake up to. Larry began to do things completely out of character, and started making irrational decisions that weren't in the best interest of our marriage.

I confronted Larry in the late fall, and we soon separated. We did not want to give up on our marriage, but over time it was quite clear Larry was not interested in making changes. We were separated for about six months before we ultimately divorced. I no longer knew the person I was once married to.

I did not want the divorce because I made a vow to God and to Larry in front of my beloved family. But after so many lies had been told and so many things had been done, I knew we couldn't recover from it. It was evident that a divorce was the only option.

Divorce is such an unwelcome word and not something that anyone plans to do when they marry but, sadly, sometimes it just can't be helped. One way I have explained divorce is that it is "completely unexpected, but absolutely necessary."

I have been sad and angry, but I can honestly say I have never been more disappointed in someone, embarrassed by someone, or ashamed of someone. Another way I describe divorce is "grieving for someone who is still living."

You may not necessarily grieve for the actual person, but instead for the things you did together.

There are so many emotions I've felt about the divorce over the years, and I think those emotions helped me realize not only that I am human, but I am an imperfect human, and it is okay to need help from time to time.

My minister recently told me how sorry he was about mine and Larry's divorce.

I responded, "I don't look at this chain of events as a setback. I view it as a setup for my comeback."

A comeback was something he had preached on months before. I hoped I would get a smile from him with that reference, and he would know I had been listening to his sermon.

Larry and I would tell each other, "God gave me you" when we dated and while we were married. I honestly believe that, and I think Larry believed it as well. We even danced to "God Gave Me You" at our wedding.

I also believe that God was taking care of me when He helped me see that the chapter of our marriage needed to end. It is so hard sometimes to understand the things that happen in life, but it is also important to remember that God has a bigger plan for us.

God has been constant throughout my separation and divorce. I was so sad and would cry and hug my puppy Oreo often after Larry moved out.

But the more I found out about the things Larry had done and decisions he had made, the less I cried.

I want to stress that I do not hate Larry, and I pray that he will turn his life around and not continue to jeopardize his relationships. He is a good person; he has just made some terrible choices.

I feel good about the place I am in now, and that is because I rely on God, my family, and my friends to help me each day. My friends and family have encouraged me more than they will ever know. They have helped me stay busy, offered help in every way possible, listened to me and offered advice, and have just been there for me when needed.

Recently, my minister has been sharing a series of sermons titled, "Unexpected." Those sermons have helped me so much. It seems like they were written just for me.

I have asked people to pray for me — and it is okay to ask people to pray for you because there are some pretty powerful prayer warriors on this earth.

I don't know what the future may hold for me, but God knows. I have faith and I don't doubt He will guide me through the rest of my days on this earth. He is my pilot and I am just a passenger. My prayers for anyone who goes through divorce are

1. That they find peace with themselves
2. That they find peace with their former spouse
3. That they rely on God and others to help them through their struggles.

I think it would be really tough to get through the unexpected events of divorce — and life in general — without those three important things.

WHEN THE BOTTOM DROPS

By C. David Farnsworth

Trust in the Lord with all thine heart, and lean not on your own understanding; in all your ways submit to Him and He will make your paths straight. (Proverbs 3:5–6)

As I shut my office door and turned off the lights, I knew I needed to be on my knees in prayer for help. For several months the employee across the hall had been causing havoc in my life. During prayer times with my once-a-week early morning men's group, I would ask them to also pray for the man whose office was only twenty-three feet away. Day after day, week after week, it seemed there was no answer from God.

Realizing I could no longer take the verbal abuse, criticism and talking behind by back, I got on my knees at the end of the work day with my hands covering my face and said, "Dear Lord, please remove this employee from our workplace or get rid of me." That was my simple prayer as I called out to God for help.

Months passed before God answered that prayer and it came in a way I did not expect. It was Thursday, January 8, a very nice winter day with temperatures in the low 60s, three days after my forty-fifth birthday. The young man who worked with me was headed to a meeting out of town so I was covering his usual public relations duties. When five o'clock rolled around I knew I needed to work a little longer, but then our general manager came for a visit and politely shut the door.

"David," he said, "beginning tomorrow we are reorganizing the company and your services will no longer be needed. Please stop what you are doing, and take this package home, and if you agree with the severance pay, sign and put it on my desk this weekend when you return to clean out your office as well as return all keys."

In shock, I asked, "Am I being fired?"

"No," he answered in a kind voice. "The company is going in a different direction and we need someone with more experience in marketing." After he continued to share the direction the company was going, I sat and listened with bewilderment. As he left my office, I continued to do some work, making phone calls I had already planned but also trying to figure out what had just happened. Within an hour the general manager returned from delivering the mail to the city post office and was concerned why I was still at the office.

He said, "David, do you need a ride home? Are you all right?"

I answered, "I'm okay."

Soon I arrived home to my wonderful wife and four beautiful daughters, trying to hold all my emotions together. I ate supper and helped put the girls to bed. But around ten o'clock as we prepared for bed, I broke down and cried as I told my wife I no longer had a job. She was so comforting as we talked about what had just happened in our lives.

When morning arrived, I did just as the general manager had mentioned in our conversation the afternoon before.

He said, "Be strong, David, as you share with your daughters that everything is going to be alright, but daddy no longer has a job." I also called a good friend to come over as we prayed for God to take care of my family.

The following day, I decided to attend the men's prayer group from our church realizing how much I needed God's help for my family and me. As I listened to these men share prayer requests, I was hesitant to speak because of pride and shame knowing these men were all successful. But as we were about to leave after praying I humbled myself and with tears in my eyes told of my recent job loss.

Immediately this loving group of men comforted and prayed for me, sharing that they were willing to do whatever their brother in Christ needed. Later that day my wife and I traveled to the office to clean out my desk, return all the keys and sign the necessary paperwork accepting my severance pay.

Beginning Monday of the next week, my new job was to find another job. My wife suggested I to go to the library and make it my new office. After I shared with the librarian and her assistants about my recent job loss, they became like family as they helped me research jobs in preparation for interviews. One of my friends even left a note on my car parked in front of the library saying, "Glad to see you're working today in your new office." Those were such encouraging words.

During my first week without a job, I also learned it was necessary to visit the state unemployment office in my local town to apply for unemployment compensation. This was again a humbling experience as I looked around the room seeing people who did not look like me. I considered myself a professional, and the majority of these folks looked like they came to this office regularly.

Within a few weeks I was notified I would begin receiving a weekly unemployment check for six months with one stipulation. I was told to call the state unemployment office every Thursday evening at ten o'clock and report the jobs I had been interviewing for during the past week. It was so humiliating to have to make a call to talk to a computer once a week. This also made me feel like a criminal who was on probation reporting in weekly. Once I came to grips with this government regulation I was able to continue going to the library daily researching jobs.

When lunch time arrived, I usually went home to be with my family, and many times after lunch, my wife Jan and I went on long walks. These were some of the richest times in our marriage, as we discussed deep feelings and tried to process all that was happening. I would often share how troubling it was to see men driving or walking down the street as I wondered what kinds of jobs they had while realizing I was unemployed. Boy, how that hurt each day thinking I was the only man in our city looking for a job.

As days turned into weeks and weeks into months of looking for a job, I wrote in my journal on May 27, "Today begins my 139th day of unemployment. It certainly has not been easy to travel this rocky road. Yet because of this difficult road, I have grown closer to my Lord." As I was also reading my devotion for that day from *Streams in the Desert* by L.B. Cowman, he expounded on Matthew 14:18 where Jesus says, "Bring them here to me."

Cowman says, "Firmly hold the vessels before Him, in faith and in prayer. Remain still before Him, and stop your own restless working until He begins to work. Do nothing that He Himself has not commanded you to do. Allow God time to work and He surely will. Then the very trials that threatened to overcome you with discouragement and disaster will become God's opportunity to reveal His grace and glory in your life, in ways you have never known before."

Wow, what comforting words to hear, knowing God was going to take care of my family. And God did answer my cry to Him. A few days after this the door opened to begin a temporary part-time job in politics. This increased my confidence knowing that someone in the workplace needed my services.

The real break came a few weeks later when I was offered a full-time position as the marketing director for a local bank. Thankfully, the bank allowed me to work both jobs until November when the election was held and the political job ended. Oh, how elated I was to be in the workplace again, working just down the street from my home and being known as a community banker.

I will always remember those many days of unemployment as I often felt defeated and afraid of the future. I was mentally exhausted from researching and preparing for interviews, and I called out to God each day for help.

As I began my banking job, I realized God was teaching me as he had taught English evangelist and orphanage director George Mueller the importance of surrendering it all to Jesus. I too needed to give up my love of money, my desire to be important, and all the worldly pleasures. I knew I wanted Jesus alone to be my all.

Sadly, it wasn't long before my life was back to where it was before my job loss. I was busy with work, busy with hobbies and even busy with church activities. But I did notice a change in my behavior. I began withdrawing from people. I was afraid of building close relationships with people, thinking they would hurt me again. Often times I would have outbursts of anger toward my children and wife. I was judgmental and unforgiving because nobody was meeting my expectations. During those times of increasing sin in my life, it was obvious I was no longer spending as much time with God as I had during my job loss.

After I had been working full-time at the bank a few months, God allowed another trial to enter my life. The bank merged with another bank and they no longer needed a local marketing person. I was told to find another job.

Having to begin searching for another job so soon seemed completely unfair, and I was asking God, "Why are you doing this to me and my family?" I could not understand, but one day while reading James 1:2 my eyes were opened to the meaning of, "Consider it pure joy … whenever you face trials of many kinds."

I saw God was using trials in our lives to make us seek Him. When I would get on my knees, bow my head and with a sincere heart confess my sin, I found joy in knowing that God would take care of me and my family.

On August 9, 1999, eighteen months after my initial job loss, I began a job that would last until retirement.

I was thrilled that I was paid to do something that I was passionate about and many people said, "David, this job fits you like a glove." For the rest of my career I had the opportunity each day to serve my fellow man in a job I loved.

I wish I could say once I began this job that all went well and that I trusted God completely. But that is not true. Life continues to be hard, for which I am grateful, because it drives me to my knees asking God to take care of me. As the title and words of Civilla Martin's hymn "God Will Take Care of You" says,

Be not dismayed whate'er betide,
God will take care of you;
Beneath His wings of love abide,
God will take care of you.
God will take care of you,
Through every day, o'er all the way;
He will take care of you,
God will take care of you.
Through days of toil when heart doth fail,
God will take care of you;
When dangers fierce your path assail,
God will take care of you.
All you may need He will provide,
God will take care of you;
Nothing you ask will be denied,
God will take care of you.
No matter what may be the test,
God will take care of you;
Lean, weary one, upon His breast,
God will take care of you.

Praise be to God who loves me and takes care of me!

NEVER ALONE

By Bryan Flanery

As I sit with my wife and four kids, I can't do anything but thank God that He has given me the chance to be here, thank Him that He never left me, and thank Him that He has shown me His power and love over and over again.

At twenty-one years old, I was working for a car dealership and I was an alcoholic. I would work from 10 a.m. to 10 p.m., then go to the bar until it closed. My father was an alcoholic too, and I had watched him deal with every problem life threw at him with alcohol. That was how I learned to deal with things.

I was in a relationship with a wonderful Christian woman who would later become my wife. But I was an atheist. (My wife says she met me during her rebellious stage — when she was rebelling from God. She was looking for a bad boy, and there I was.) Our differing religious views caused tension in our relationship.

I wasn't a good person at all. It wasn't because I was an atheist, I just wasn't a good person. When I met her family, they said, "What are you doing with this guy? You have to leave. He's an idiot and there's nothing godly about this man."

She wrote a note to herself back then that said, "Everybody is telling me to leave, but God is telling me to stay and watch."

I remember coming home from the bars one night and she wouldn't speak to me. She wanted nothing to do with me. I went to bed realizing if something didn't change I was going to lose her, and she was the one bright spot I ever had in my life.

I always felt I needed to be in the military. I felt the call to join the army, but I had never been encouraged to do so.

One morning, I called in sick to work and went to a nearby recruiting station to speak with the people there. People often ask me what led me to go to the recruiting station and I had no idea at the time, but looking back now, I can say without a doubt it was God.

I was offered a job as an X-ray technician. I would be a part of the army, work in a hospital taking pictures of people's bones, and never be in danger. It was perfect.

But when I was at one of the visits for the army, the guy in front of me couldn't pick a job and they were showing him videos of all the possible army careers. I'm watching the videos too, and I see a guy shove a huge round into a cannon and watch the explosion flatten this wooded area. I knew then that I didn't need to be an X-ray technician. I wanted to work in combat artillery.

I broke the news to my friends and family at a barbeque. I had told my wife that I was interviewing for a general manager position at a new dealership in Arizona to cover for my trips for the army. Everyone at the barbeque was expecting me to announce that I got the general manager position and we would be moving to Arizona.

When everyone arrived, I stood on a barstool so everyone could see me clearly and I said, "Well, I'm going to be moving. And just so you know, I'm moving to Georgia." Everyone stopped and looked at me surprised. "I went down to the recruiting station, and I enlisted in the Army." As soon as I said it, my dad came running across the yard and leveled me off the barstool and started yelling at me. It's safe to say that no one was thrilled by my announcement. But as everyone was lining up to yell at me, I saw a smile come across my wife's face. I walked to her and grabbed her hand and promised her this wasn't an impulse decision.

"It'll be all right," she said, hugging me.

"I hope so," I said. "Because you're going to be an army wife." She started laughing because, at that time, we were still dating. But the next weekend, I took her out and proposed. She said "yes," and I left for basic training the next week.

We got married the day I got back from basic training. She planned the whole thing while I was away. My buddy picked me up from the airport and told me we were headed to my wedding.

It was a cool moment because my wedding was the first time I got to see all my friends and family since I left for basic training. It was a special time.

After the birth of our first child, I was moved to Fort Campbell, Kentucky, and was quickly deployed to Kandahar, Afghanistan — one of the most dangerous places on earth. I was so excited, but I didn't really understand the danger I was moving into.

Our mission in Kandahar was to retake control of the area from the Taliban. One night I was on nighttime overwatch and I hurt my knee. I was put in the back of a truck with a few other guys and we headed back to the airfield. We were jamming to music on one guy's laptop when everything went black. The truck was forced off the road, the driver lost control, and we rolled down a ravine. No one, including me, realized how bad my injuries were.

When I was injured, I had no connection with any higher being. I didn't believe in Christ or Buddha or anybody.

I came home and things got worse and worse. I was having things taken out of my neck and things put into my hips and shoulders and knees. People kept saying, "After this you'll be better." But when the better never came, I started hearing things like, "This is your new normal, get used to this" instead. What people didn't see outside of the physical struggles is that I went into a deep pit of depression.

I was moved into the Warrior Transition Battalion, where soldiers are either integrated back into the force or transitioned into civilian life. Shortly after starting there, they told me there wasn't anything else they could do to improve my injuries and I would be retired. All I knew was how to be a soldier, and now, that was taken away from me. I could never be what I once was. I couldn't be the father I once was. Playing with my kids hurt. I couldn't be the husband my wife deserved. All of these changes pushed me to a deeper level of hopelessness.

I heard a guy recently say that when someone is considering suicide the first thing you should do is remind them of their family. If someone had walked into my room and told me to think of my family, I would've said, "Who the heck do you think I'm doing this for?" I thought if I couldn't be the man my family deserved, the least I could do would be to leave them some money from my life insurance, so they could go on with their life without worrying about money.

When you wake up every morning and the people around you are telling you that there is no hope, no way to get better, then what's the point of waking up in the first place? That's what led to the suicide attempt: not having hope that anything could change.

I was mad at the world, but I didn't want my wife or kids to find me. They didn't deserve that. I moved my wife and kids back to Indiana under the false pretense that she could get a head start finding a house and a job after my retirement.

The whole time I knew I was going to take my life, and my one fear was that my wife and kids would be the ones to find me. So, I swallowed two bottles of pills.

But God wasn't done with me. One of my neighbors came over to my room to ask if I wanted to play video games, and he found me. He jumped into action and he helped save my life. I know it was a God thing because the guy and I never hung out, but that night he came over to my room.

I almost forced my wife to raise two children on her own and let them wonder if it was their fault. I can't imagine the pain I would've caused.

At the time I thought suicide was the right choice for my kids, but I can't imagine as they got older and really realized what happened, what that would do to them. Christ can heal all things, but I can't fathom the pain I would've caused my wife and kids. At the time, my logic was so sound that my death was what was best for them, but now our other two children are so amazing and so funny, and who knows what their futures hold. They could do something that impacts the whole world or just one person for the Kingdom, and I almost took that away.

I'm now eight years removed from my injury and everyday is still a struggle as far as physical pain. At thirty-two, I have severe back and neck pain. For a long time, the doctor treated my pain with opiates. It wasn't until December 2017 that I made the decision not to take them anymore. They weren't really helping me. They were just masking the pain, and I was becoming addicted to them.

When you're at a high level of pain and you take something that reduces it just a little bit, it's easy to want to continue to take them just to have that release. Now, I treat my pain with exercise, acupuncture, stretching, and yoga.

I still live in a high level of pain. The biggest difference between then and now is that I now know there is hope. Now I know that pain doesn't define who I am, and my identity isn't rooted in the fact that I'm a disabled veteran or that I was a service member.

My identity is rooted in Christ and what He did for me. I'm not who people say I am or think I am. I am who Christ says I am. I know what Scripture says about me. I am perfectly made. The biggest change in my pain isn't necessarily the pain level but how I view the pain.

I'm not a billionaire or a millionaire. I'm just a guy that works for a non-profit trying to help others get through the worst days of their life. At the end of the day, the one thing that I can give my wife and kids is time.

If I had been successful, I would never be able to give them that time. When I was in the middle of suffering, I isolated myself from my wife and kids and people in general.

Now it's not an inconvenience to just sit down and read or play Legos. It changed the way I speak. It changed the way I view the world. It changed everything. It helped me see that there is a purpose and hope. I'm starting to see what His purpose for me was.

Reboot Alliance, which helps veterans and first responders through faith-based PTSD and trauma recovery is where I accepted Christ and where I began healing from all my past hurts.

Now I work for Reboot Alliance, and I have the pleasure of traveling around the country sharing my story and helping other veterans see that suicide is not the answer and God is not the cause of the problem, but the solution. God has never fired a firearm; He's never loaded a cannon or thrown a grenade. He's never done anything like that. Sinful man has done those things. As a whole, you can see that God has used man's greatest sin to produce good.

I look back and some of the worst seasons ended up being when I've grown the most. I think about in Matthew when the disciples are on the ship and it's storming and Jesus is asleep at the helm, then He wakes up and goes out onto the deck and says, "Peace, be still," and as soon as He utters those words, the waves stop.

And for most of us, we don't even realize we are in the storm. Even when we are in the storm, Jesus is right there with us and no storm is bigger than Christ. But that storm produced so much fruit. That story was when the disciples realized who He was. In that one storm, the disciples went from thinking they were going to die and it was the worst day of their lives, to it being the best day of their lives because they realized they are walking with God.

For anybody going through the storm, know there is a way out. And it can't be found in a bottle or through suicide. Suicide is a permanent solution to a temporary problem. You're not ending the pain, you're just shifting the pain from one person to another.

The only way out of a storm is through Christ. Even in the darkest night, even in the middle of the storm, He is with me. His people are with me. We are never alone.

DOUBLE PORTION

By Rhonda Hayes

When I got married at twenty-one years old I thought I was marrying my sweetheart and that it would last forever. But sometimes we are dealt cards we don't want or ask for.

I was married to my husband for twenty years.

Our marriage wasn't perfect, but nothing was so bad that I didn't think we couldn't work on it or that God couldn't fix it. But when only one person is trying or wanting it to work, it's really difficult.

I did not want a divorce. I prayed and dug into God's Word more than I had ever done before. I memorized Scripture that spoke to me. I taped verses on my mirror, the refrigerator, on the dash of my car.

I tried to do everything I possibly could to show my husband I loved him no matter what and show him we could fix our mess.

I wouldn't wish divorce on my worst enemy. It is definitely the most devastating experience I have ever gone through in my life.

The worst part of all was how it tore apart our nine-year-old daughter's life. The children are just innocent bystanders in the situation, but their lives are impacted greatly.

I told God one day that I really didn't want to live the rest of my life alone, but I would if it meant that my daughter would not have to endure any more heartache. I told God if He had a good, godly man who would treat me and my daughter like queens, He would have to drop him in my path.

I stayed very involved with my church, my family, and my daughter's activities. Staying busy and positive was very important to me. If anyone was negative, I shied away from them.

My husband and I were separated for five years. Everywhere I went I felt like people talked about me, felt sorry for me, or just thought I was crazy. My own mother even said, "Why don't you just move on with your life?" That was so much easier said than done.

At this point I vowed to be careful when judging others. If you don't know the whole story or you haven't been there, it's best to keep your mouth closed and just pray for them instead.

After five years of separation, we finally divorced and I found infidelity was the deep-rooted seed, though he never admitted it to me.

I told God I didn't understand why I had to go through this; however, I wanted to be able to use my horrible experience one day to help someone else who might need to hear it.

God has opened that door numerous times for me to share.

One year after my divorce God brought a wonderful godly man into my life that already knew my daughter very well. He was a teacher at her school. He has been a true Godsend to me. He definitely treats us both like queens. Even now after she is married with two kids, he still treats us both like royalty.

I stand on the verse in Genesis 50:20 that says, "You intended to harm me, but God intended it for good..." He restored me with double of what I had before.

Isaiah 61:7 says it best: "Instead of your shame you will receive a double portion, and instead of disgrace you will rejoice in your inheritance. And so you will inherit a double portion in your land, and everlasting joy will be yours."

Those verses, and many others, helped me so much during my loneliest times. To this day, when I read them or run across them, I smile with such a comfort in my heart. God is so faithful to us. Lean on Him during your problems and I promise you He will bring you through it and you will be a better person on the other side.

I still struggle with forgiveness to this day. It is very hard for me to totally forgive my ex-husband and the other woman, whom he is now married to, but with God's help I believe I will be able to overcome that one day.

I know unforgiveness doesn't hurt them, but only me. I have to ask God daily to help me with this and it gets easier each day. There is another verse that sums up my story: 1 Peter 1:6–7. It says, "In all this you greatly rejoice, though now for a little while you may have had to suffer grief in all kinds of trials. These have come so that the proven genuineness of your faith — of greater worth than gold which perishes even though refined by fire — may be proved genuine and may result in praise, glory, and honor when Jesus Christ is revealed."

GOD IS IN CONTROL

By Jeff Helms

Where do you turn when your wife, through tears and excruciating pain, shares what she fears may be her final request?

"Take care of our daughter, and make sure our son knows Jesus and how much God loves him," Laurie said as we sped toward the emergency room.

How do you respond to such a plea? Where do you look to find strength?

"I lift up my eyes to the mountains — Where does my help come from? My help comes from the Lord, the Maker of heaven and earth" (Psalm 121:1–2).

For Laurie and me, the only place to turn on January 31, 2016, was our sovereign Lord.

It was a Sunday, like any other. Laurie was helping with the sixth-grade class. I was studying First and Second Peter in the adult wing.

Then, deep inside Laurie's brain something happened that would reset our priorities, refocus our perspective, and refine our faith.

A four-millimeter aneurysm — the thickness of two nickels — ruptured. Intense pain, unlike she'd ever experienced, gripped Laurie's body, bringing nausea and numbness to her leg.

Laurie stumbled from the supply room where she was copying activity sheets and fell into the loving arms of a church elder.

Our preacher's wife found me, and I ran to Laurie's side. More elders gathered around her to pray as I retrieved our vehicle before speeding away to a nearby hospital.

As we drove those endless miles, Laurie had one request. "Make sure our son keeps loving the Lord."

You see, our daughter has Down syndrome, and we know where she'll spend eternity. So, in that moment, a mother's love was focused not on her health, not on financial security, not even on physical safety, but rather on her son's spiritual future.

"Lord, give me strength. I know you'll take care of us no matter what. You always have, but please let Laurie be okay."

As a journalist, I should have more profound words — a more eloquent prayer. But as I looked into the eyes of my wife, the pain, uncertainty, and fear descended on my brain like a fog. My vision narrowed as I searched for direction until all I could focus on was Laurie and the Lord.

I stumbled for words of encouragement and prayers of hope. Unable to formulate complex thoughts and sentences, I leaned on the Holy Spirit.

"Speak for me, Spirit. Lord, You know my heart. Help me. Help Laurie."

Little did I know, God already was demonstrating His sovereignty.

Five days earlier, Laurie had an intense headache as I was preparing for work. It scared her, but soon subsided into a dull, lingering pain.

The doctors called it a sentinel bleed. I say it was God preparing us for Sunday morning.

"Don't wait. This is serious," were the Spirit's urgent prompts that morning.

As I fought the panic rising in my gut, God directed us to the right hospital.

According to Google Maps, our church is between 3.4 and 6 miles from three hospitals. Which one was the best option for a brain aneurysm at 9:45 on a Sunday morning?

The elder who held Laurie as I pulled the truck to the church door suggested an emergency room about five minutes away.

When we arrived, observant nurses quickly recognized Laurie's stroke-like symptoms and expedited triage. Within minutes, we met the doctor who quite possibly saved Laurie's life.

Remember it's Sunday morning. So, who would we expect to see? Certainly not the director of the emergency department who, by the way, previously worked in a military head injury clinic.

Unless, you believe God is in control. Then, a wise and experienced physician is exactly what you'd expect.

But God didn't stop there.

He helped this doctor look beyond the easy diagnosis of a migraine and order a CT scan and MRI.

The tests confirmed our fears. Laurie would be transported by helicopter to a larger hospital. But which one?

Alabama's No. 1 hospital was extremely busy and had been diverting patients for weeks.

Again, God provided a way.

Laurie's ER doctor just so happened to be friends with the father of the chief resident of neurosurgery at our preferred hospital. A phone call later, Laurie was on her way.

On the MedEvac flight, Laurie clung to the sovereignty of our God.

"... Salvation belongs to our God who sits on the throne, and to the Lamb." (Revelation 7:10)

As the sound of the rotors drowned out the world, Laurie heard these words over and over in her mind.

"God is in control. No matter what, He wins. He is our hope, our salvation."

Meanwhile, I was making the longest two-hour drive of my life. Friends often say, "I bet you flew up the interstate!"

Quite the opposite. I proceeded carefully, prayerfully — remembering the words of my wife.

"Take care of our kids."

At the hospital, we were continually reminded of God's goodness.

"Because of the Lord's great love we are not consumed, for His compassions never fail. They are new every morning; great is your faithfulness" (Lamentations 3:22–23).

Surgery was scheduled for Monday morning, but Sunday night, God sent us an attentive nurse who recognized Laurie was in distress.

Spinal fluid wasn't circulating correctly, and the building pressure in Laurie's brain cavity threatened to push her into a coma.

More scans were ordered, and a drain was placed inside Laurie's brain to relieve the pressure.

During surgery, the aneurysm ruptured again, requiring additional titanium clips to stem the bleeding, and an optic nerve had to be moved, threatening blurred or double vision.

To meet these challenges, God provided skilled doctors and nurses. By the time Laurie was brought back to the ICU, she was talking.

Less than twenty-four hours later, she was eating grits and eggs.

Dozens of Christian friends visited, and countless prayers were offered on Laurie's behalf.

Coworkers bowed their heads at my office, our son's school gathered for prayer, and congregations of friends, family and total strangers added Laurie to their care lists.

For eight days, we made prayer requests from ICU. We asked that Laurie not suffer a dangerous vasospasm. We pleaded for her to avoid needing a permanent shunt. And, we prayed for the families around us — some dealing with unimaginable trauma.

God answered — sometimes in ways we expected and other times with a wondrous surprise.

One afternoon, our neighbor in the ICU was gripped mid-sentence with a paralyzing seizure. She was a liver transplant patient who contracted pneumonia and was placed on the neurological floor so she would have around-the-clock care.

She wasn't supposed to be there. Now, I was watching fear and confusion fill eyes that moments before sparkled with anticipation of health and home.

But God had a plan.

You see, one of my coworkers' mother-in-law also suffered seizures following a liver transplant. God reminded me of that later in the evening.

By then, our neighbor had been through a battery of scans and tests. Laurie and I were praying for her, as were some of our closest friends. But there were no answers.

That is, until God woke me from a semi-conscious nap with a vague memory. A quick text to my coworker confirmed anti-rejection drugs had caused similar symptoms in her mother-in-law.

Tentatively, I approached our nurse with the discovery. And to God's glory, instead of dismissing my amateur diagnosis, he asked for more information. Additional texts yielded the names of medications and, after adjustments were made to prescriptions, our neighbor's seizures ceased.

"For my thoughts are not your thoughts, neither are your ways my ways, declares the Lord" (Isaiah 55:8).

Laurie recovered.

Fully. Gloriously.

No therapy. No medicine. No deficiencies.

Nine days. Three titanium clips. Fifty staples. Thousands of prayers.

One unanswered question.

Why?

Why were our prayers answered?

During our marriage, Laurie and I have prayed fervently for healing, reconciliation and recovery for faithful brothers and sisters.

We've seen God do amazing things. But we've also wrestled to accept why, at other times, He didn't provide an earthly cure.

It's at once humbling and convicting. We are reminded that nothing is special about our faith or prayers, and yet we are challenged to make it count.

Like the captain's final admonition in "Saving Private Ryan:" "Earn this!"

So, that's what we are trying to do. With each day and each response to Laurie's healing, we seek to give God the glory.

He has been, and always will be, who we look to for help.

"If the Lord had not been on our side ... the flood would have engulfed us, the torrent would have swept over us" (Psalm 124:1, 4).

I LOVE YOU SON

By Randy Helms

I was fortunate enough to have been born into a Christian home. My formative years were centered around church, family, and community. Like everyone else, along the way I experienced disappointments, hurts, and challenges. But I was always taught to rely on my faith, and God would see me through those difficult times.

Following college graduation, I accepted a grant-funded job that was supposed to last twelve months. Nearly forty years later, I am the director of that same organization. Along the way I met Lisa, the woman who would later become my wife. We enjoyed life to the fullest, and we were soon blessed with our daughter Hayden. Three years later, we were blessed once again when our son Hunter was born. God truly smiled down on us with the two most wonderful children He ever created. We loved being a family and making memories together. Life had been so good to me.

But on the afternoon of Friday, May 4, 2012, my world was changed forever. Two of our close friends and one of our pastors appeared at our house and delivered the three words that will haunt me forever.

"He's passed away."

As the shock of those words penetrated my being I was sure that there was no way that this could be right. There had to be some type of misunderstanding, some kind of mistake.

Hunter was the son every father hopes for. He was all boy, and he enjoyed life and all things masculine. As a family we had always admired his integrity and his refusal to participate in gossip. Lisa and I had often wondered how he could be so morally mature at such a young age. Hunter stayed dedicated to sports and school, and he never struggled with discipline issues.

I enjoyed many firsts with him: hitting his first homerun, scoring his first touchdown, catching his first fish, harvesting his first deer and gobbler, witnessing his elation at his sixteenth birthday party when he received his first vehicle, and watching him fall in love for the first time. He was my son, my outdoors partner, and my best buddy.

Hunter had graduated from high school the previous year, and he had just finished his freshman year at Shelton State Community College in Tuscaloosa, Alabama. He had been home the previous weekend, and we had enjoyed turkey hunting and playing basketball together. Little did I know that when we gave each other our customary bear hug on Sunday afternoon before he headed back to school that it would be our last.

Friends drove Lisa, Hayden, and me to Tuscaloosa where we were taken to the police department. Since Hunter had passed away at his residence, a death investigation had been conducted. We were informed by the investigators that Hunter had gone to sleep the previous night and never woken up.

As we began preparations for Hunter's funeral, it was all beginning to become real. The visitation was held on Sunday afternoon with an unbelievable 750 friends and family attending. The following afternoon the sanctuary of our church was filled for his funeral. We were humbled by the outpouring of love and support.

For the next several days, Lisa, Hayden, and I were in complete shock. At best, I was sleeping two hours a night. Both of my parents were in their eighties, and I felt the need to be the rock of the family and to support my parents, Lisa, and Hayden as they grieved.

We had been involved in a small group Bible study for a number of years, and it was these close friends who walked with us and gave us the much needed day-to-day support that was vital to our emotional and mental stability. As reality was setting in, I began to analyze what had happened and how I would respond. And I had so many questions.

The first question I asked myself was whether or not I believed Hunter's death was God's fault. As I debated this question in my mind, it was clear that there were two paths for the future:

1) If God was to blame for Hunter's death, then the Christian faith that I had practiced for many years was all a sham. It meant that life on earth is all there is and eternity does not exist. It meant that I would live out the remainder of my life as a bitter and hopeless man.

Or, 2) God did not cause this to happen, He only allowed it to happen. If I truly believed in a loving God, I could have the peace of knowing that Hunter was experiencing heaven. I knew that if I ever had any hopes of seeing my son again, this was the only option available. It was at this point that I committed to not harboring any bitterness toward God.

My second question was why did this have to happen to Hunter instead of me. I had lived a full life. I had attained the highest position in my profession. I traveled, got married, and had a family, checked off many bucket list items, and was much older than he was. So why?

The answer came as it has only a few times in my lifetime; God spoke to me so clearly that I could not mistake it for anything else.

The answer was this: "If it had been you rather than Hunter, he would be experiencing the same grief as you. Because he was so much younger, he would have many more years on the earth to grieve. Would you rather Hunter go through the torment of grief for many more years, or would you rather grieve in his place knowing that he's with Me in heaven?" It was almost as if God was showing me the correlation of allowing Jesus to die on the cross in my place. I determined that I would rather take on the grief as opposed to having Hunter suffer with it. This was a game changer for me.

At this point, I wanted to know what Hunter was experiencing, so I began purchasing books on heaven. A common thread of every book I read is that it's a place that's so incredible that words just aren't adequate enough to describe what awaits us. I gained a degree of comfort knowing that Hunter was in such an awesome place.

Six months after Hunter passed away, my father suffered a brain hemorrhage and died five days later. In the span of six months I had lost the two most important males in my life. I continued reading about heaven and other books related to loss. I remained determined that I would not allow myself to be bitter.

As my readings, my prayers, and the comfort from my close friends and family sustained me, I was acutely aware of God's presence. As a family we began to notice little things that would have been so easy to dismiss as coincidences; however, we were sure that it was God speaking to us. Two of those moments stand out particularly.

Five weeks after Hunter's death, Lisa and I were having a bad day. It was a Saturday and we decided to get out for a while. On our way home, I decided to stop by the post office. The post office was closed for business and I was the only person in the building. Lisa had given me a cup to throw in the garbage drum inside. As I approached the drum I could tell that the garbage bag had recently been changed.

As I was about to toss the cup in I noticed there was only one other item in the drum. Because of the amount of air under the new bag, the item was lodged in the top of the drum. As I looked closer I realized it looked like a picture of Hunter. I pulled the item out and it was in fact Hunter's picture. It was the program for his funeral with his photograph on the front. When I returned to the car and handed it to Lisa, I wondered aloud what it meant.

Without hesitation, she responded, "It means he's with us." In the days that followed, I tried to logically make sense of this event. It had been five weeks since the funeral. The program looked as if it had just been printed. There were no wrinkles, dog ears, or stains of any kind. It was if it had been placed in the top of the drum just for me. This raised so many questions: How could it be in such pristine condition if it had been in someone's vehicle for five weeks? Why did someone wait that long to dispose of it? What were the odds that I would stop at the post office on a Saturday afternoon? What were the odds that I would find it? To this day I'm at a loss for an explanation; however, I'm confident that it was not a coincidence.

The second event that I will share occurred with Hunter's girlfriend Lexi. They met in Tuscaloosa and had been dating for several months. Lexi visited our home often and she was considered a part of the family. Several weeks after Hunter died, Lexi received a telephone call on her cell phone from the number that had once belonged to Hunter. Apparently she had butt dialed Hunter's number and the new owner of the number was returning the missed call. As the conversation progressed, Lexi learned that the last name of the new owner of Hunter's number was Heavens. Is this another coincidence? I think not.

As the weeks turned into months, we did our best to make sense of our changed lives. We leaned on our small group and church family for support, comfort, and reassurance.

In one of my readings, I came across a quote from Rick Warren, who had also suffered the loss of a son.

He said, "Your greatest tragedy may be your greatest ministry." This quote began to become a reality for both Lisa and me. Lisa and I had both experienced the seventy-two hour Walk to Emmaus a few years earlier, and we stayed involved in different capacities.

Lisa was asked to participate in an upcoming ladies walk and to talk to the group. I had no idea how she was going to be able to share her faith and her loss in a group setting. I received feedback from several of the ladies who were present for her talk and they were in awe of the impact that her words had.

Now it was my turn. Boyd Deal, the mind behind this book, contacted me a few weeks prior to Father's Day in 2013. He asked me to pray about sharing my story with his church on Father's Day. My initial reaction was that since this would be my first Father's Day without both my son and my dad, there was simply no way that I could honor his request. Following much prayer, I felt an unusual peace and against my better judgment I agreed to speak.

I have often heard preachers and others who have spoken in churches make the statement that words came out of their mouths that were not planned. I can be added to that list. My prayers were answered and I was able to keep most of my emotions in check. I felt God's presence while I spoke, and I was convinced that I was honoring Him.

Several years ago, I was asked to participate in a men's leadership group at church. Joshua's Men is a group of twelve men who agreed to participate in a year-long course to enhance leadership skills. Our church later partnered with another large Methodist church to implement the same program.

The course always begins with an out-of-town weekend retreat. I have been asked to share my story with several of these groups during the past several years during their retreat. I have used my experience to illustrate the frailties that we as men are confronted with. I've also challenged them to surround themselves with a support group of godly men who will walk with them through the dark times that we all face. I also shared the following story and explained how God has put it on my heart to share with every group I speak to.

As we were going through Hunter's possessions that were in his room in Tuscaloosa, there were several pages of schoolwork in a drawer. One item appeared to be a paper that he had written for his first semester English course. The title of the paper was "My Role Model." I'm sure this was not a topic that he selected, rather it was probably the standard subject matter for all students. As I began to read the words that he had penned about *me*, tears filled my eyes. He mentioned many of the wonderful experiences the two of us had shared, as well as some of the values that I had instilled in him.

Hunter could not have left a more precious gift for me. After reading through the paper several times in the following days and reflecting on the things that were said, it was as if I received a knee to the stomach. From nowhere there was a realization that the paper could have been about someone other than me. What if it had been about one of his coaches, his youth pastor, a friend's dad, or anyone else? That feeling still haunts me. I will forever remain thankful that I impacted Hunter in a positive light. As I've shared this with the men's groups that I've spoken to, I've stressed that regardless of their relationships with their children, and regardless of the ages, they should do everything within their power to make sure the paper would be about them. Would your child's paper be about you?

Never in my wildest imagination did I think that Lisa and I would be navigating this life without one of our children. Needless to say, our lives have been forever altered.

As we will all face crises in one form or another, the most important question becomes how will we respond?

Will we place the blame on God and live a bitter and resentful life, or will we place our faith in God? We've chosen to trust God to comfort us in this life, knowing that we will be reunited with Hunter for eternity. I sincerely hope that as you face life's challenges, you trust in the One who gives us all hope and comfort.

Written in honor of Hunter Charles Helms. I love you son!

IMMEASURABLY MORE

By Dell Hill

James Mallory left Madison County, Virginia, with his and several other families in April 1834. In May, they arrived in Huntsville, Alabama, where they would spend the summer. In October, all the families moved and settled in the Alpine area of Talladega County. James Mallory's land was named Selwood and it still carries that name today. Selwood remained in Mallory's family until purchased by my parents in 1948.

My father, O.V. Hill, was the county agent in Talladega County, and was constantly looking for ways to improve the life and income of the farmers in the area. Through the years, all types of livestock and fowl were raised at Selwood. Eventually turkeys and brood cows became the main commodities.

As a way to add value to the farm product, we started smoking turkeys. This quickly led to a small mail order business. The process of raising, smoking, and selling turkeys continued until Daddy died in 1968.

I met my wife, Carolyn, at Auburn University and we were married in 1965. I spent two years in the Army, and then we moved to Decatur where I was employed as a chemical engineer and Carolyn taught school. Life was good. We made friends and enjoyed a full social calendar. After Daddy's death we moved to Talladega to continue the business and farm. The move to Talladega brought us back to my home church where we quickly got involved and even took on leadership roles.

In the fall of 1971, our church invited twenty laypeople to spend a week in our church sharing their Christian stories. This group included housewives, businessmen, professionals, and retirees visiting in our homes and worshipping with us. After hearing their personal testimonies, Carolyn and I realized that we were not Christians and that Christ had been missing in our marriage and family. After six years of marriage, we knelt and prayed together and asked Christ into our hearts and lives. Following our church's revival, Carolyn and I became actively involved in several church revivals around Alabama and in other states where we shared our Christian testimony. Our lives grew more stable and our faith grew stronger.

Over the next ten years we built a home on Selwood land, had two children, and expanded the mail order business and cattle business. Each of these endeavors involved borrowing money. The land was used as collateral to secure the loan. Until the early 1980s all went well. The businesses were profitable enough to service the debt and enjoy a comfortable lifestyle.

All of that changed in 1982. From 1982 to 1984 we hit several bad cattle markets and by 1984 we were $250,000 in debt. The bank was advertising a courthouse sale of the land. We attempted to negotiate with the bank to work through the issue, but the talks were fruitless and a sale was scheduled for the next week. Feeling helpless we were resigned to letting events play out.

Numerous emotions flooded my mind and spirit as I calculated the future of my family and the farm that I had treasured since I was a small boy.

Where would we live? How could I make a living? How could I overcome the large farm debt? Who would gain ownership of our family farm? Was I wrong in believing it was the Lord leading us to move to the farm and seek livelihood from the produce of the land?

There was an incident during that trying period when Carolyn was en route to attend a ladies' conference in Montgomery. As she drove, our situation was swirling through her mind. She was fearful, worried, and very fretful as her foot pushed heavily on the accelerator. Suddenly she saw the dreaded flashing light of a highway patrolman behind her. As she pulled over, she burst into uncontrollable tears. When the patrolman got to the window, rather than threatening her, he gently spoke calming words and asked her to gain her composure and then continue slowly. She realized that the Lord was watching over her.

Carolyn and I realized that we frequently operated on our own strength, and made plans for the future without praying together. We started asking what we should do and for the direction for our future. We decided to trust God, asking daily for wisdom and guidance. A number of our Christian friends offered prayers, wisdom, and anonymous financial assistance. Peace returned to our lives as we walked by faith.

On Tuesday prior to the sale date, a man we knew got a particle of trash in his eye and visited an ophthalmologist friend of ours. In conversation, the doctor relayed our situation to his patient, Mr. Jones, knowing that he knew us and also had interest in land. In addition the doctor thought that Mr. Jones could possibly help. Mr. Jones called me and I described our situation. He came out to Selwood, we talked, and I told him if we sold some of the land we could possibly manage the remaining debt, and could continue our businesses.

He made no commitments, only saying, "Let me see what I can do." Another close friend of ours was connected to the local bank branch as well as the home office. His phone calls paved the way for a conversation between Mr. Jones and the bank. On a phone call, the bank cancelled our farm sale and sold Mr. Jones the note at face value. He then became the lender of record.

Yes, we still had a large debt, but we had time to work our way out of debt, and in time we fully repaid the entire amount. What seemed to be an impossible situation really was not. All because of a particle of trash in someone's eye.

In all of this we realized that if we wanted to stay on the land, we needed to do some things differently. After prayer for direction and vision, in 1984 and 1990 we started Selwood Hunting Preserve and Selwood Sporting Clays.

Selwood is now completely recreational, hosting 10,000–12,000 visitors a year. We offer the finest in shotgun sports and wing shooting. In 1984 we were told that people would not pay to hunt because "there is too much free land". Possibly true then, but land uses have changed dramatically since then and many venues similar to Selwood have opened in the state.

In the years since those early difficulties, Carolyn and I have seen God do "immeasurably more than all we ask or imagine, according to His power that is at work within us" (Ephesians 3:20).

AT MY SAVIOR'S FEET

By Pam Hughes

My struggle began in 1998, approximately three months after my husband accepted Jesus and I re-dedicated my life to the Lord.

It didn't take long for Satan to begin his attack on our family. It happened just as we made the decision to live our lives for the Lord, and raise our children in the admonition of God. But this attack came as no surprise to God.

He knew exactly what was about to happen in our lives, and He knew that we would desperately need Him in the days, months, and years to come. He prepared us in His perfect timing to accept His perfect grace so He could walk with us through the struggle that was ahead.

You see, three months after we committed our lives to the Lord, we found out that my baby brother, who was ten years younger than me, was battling a severe addiction to crack cocaine.

My baby brother was only fifteen years old at the time, so this was devastating news to our entire family. Needless to say, we were in shock and denial at the time. We had no idea how severe his addiction was.

We had no idea what challenges our family would face. We had no experience with this sort of problem; we simply had no idea what to do.

I remember my entire family feeling hopeless, hurt, and scared to death. I also remember falling on my knees daily praying for strength and for healing from this addiction for my brother. I found comfort in God's Word and His promises to us, but if I am truthful, sometimes it seemed like the more I prayed, the worse the situation got.

I believed then and I still believe now that nothing makes God happier than someone on their knees in prayer, and nothing makes Satan angrier. So I prayed and prayed and prayed.

I prayed for divine intervention, healing, and restoration for my brother and my entire family. It didn't come. It appeared as though Satan was winning the battle. My little brother, Brian, would go to rehab, clean up for a few weeks, and then relapse. Time and time again, he would give in to the hold crack cocaine had on him.

Sure, our family was closer than we had ever been. After all, we were walking through hell on earth together. Our daily lives were filled with the fear of what could be next.

We went through times of not knowing where Brian was for weeks at a time to finally being relieved when we would get a call that he was in jail. If he was in jail at least he was alive, and we knew where he was even if only for a few days. It's a sad thing to feel relieved that someone you love is in jail. But I remember feeling that way many, many days. A vicious cycle of diversion center, rehab, and jail was Brian's life as well as ours.

Even though we were going through indescribable heartache during those years, my family was closer in those days than ever before. Every chance we had to tell Brian we loved him, we told him. We never knew if we would get that chance again. We supported, encouraged, and helped him in any way we could. We probably even enabled him some.

Tough love is called "tough" for a reason. Because it is tough. Brian knew his family loved him, he knew we supported him, and he knew we always had his best interest at heart no matter what we had to do. Sometimes we had to make hard decisions that seemed to hurt Brian to try to help him.

By the age of nineteen, Brian was married, shortly afterward separated, and had a baby girl named Kayla. My parents were raising Kayla, but Brian was an active part of her life as much as we could allow him to be. We hoped and prayed that having a baby girl would give him the willpower to stay clean, but again we were ignorant to the fact that a crack cocaine addiction doesn't care if he has a baby girl.

We watched as Brian tried so hard to beat his addiction. Truthfully, sometimes I just got mad with him for not being strong enough, and for putting our family through this turmoil.

Looking back now, I know Brian didn't mean to put us through that, and he was hurting and struggling just as much we were. He was as helpless over himself as we were over him.

I think people who have never experienced this sort of thing have no understanding of how sick and desperate the addict is. Yes, it may have been their choice in the beginning to try the drug, but nobody intends to become an addict. Nobody plans to have their life and family ripped apart by an addiction. It takes you completely by surprise.

One bad decision can affect the rest of your life and the lives of those that you love. Just one bad decision is all it takes. That one split second decision that Brian made to try drugs for the first time sent him into a seven-year-long, battle for his life. He battled every single day of his life from fifteen to twenty-one years old.

During one of Brian's many incarcerations, my father-in-law, who participated in a local jail inmate visitation ministry on Monday nights, prayed with my brother to receive Christ. One Monday night, my father-in-law saw Brian in jail and he was able to share the plan of salvation with him, and Brian accepted Jesus as his Lord and Savior.

I will never forget my father-in-law calling me to tell me that Brian had been saved. He knew Brian personally, and he was confident that Brian's salvation experience was sincere and heartfelt.

Oh, what an answered prayer. After all this time, I was sure that God was going to deliver Brian and our family from the torment we were living in. He would divinely heal him from this addiction so that he could have a testimony as to what God can and will do in your life. I was so excited for what God was doing in and through Brian.

Once Brian was released from jail, he came back home to live with our mother. He was reading his Bible and told our mother that he needed to go buy some church clothes because he was going back to church.

Brian had been in and out of church most of his life, but had not been faithfully attending. I was excited to see what God's calling on Brian's life would be. I knew he would be able to minister to so many people who may be struggling with the same issues. However, Brian would not get the chance to buy those church clothes. He would not get the chance to go back to church. He would not get the chance to be baptized because Brian was killed in a head-on collision on March 16, 2005, at approximately 9:25 p.m.

At just twenty-one years old, my baby brother was gone. I will never forget the night that the Sheriff's Department called my house around midnight.

The deputy said, "Pam, I need you to come to your dad's house." Of course, being the insistent person that I am, I demanded he tell me what was wrong.

He simply said, "It's your brother."

I asked, "Is he okay?"

He replied, "No he's not okay, please come to your dad's house." Half asleep and scared to death, I managed to drive to my dad's house where I was confronted with the heartbreaking news that my brother had been instantly killed in a head-on collision.

The hours, days, and months ahead were filled with tears, anger, and many hopeless thoughts and feelings. I was so mad. I was furious at God.

Reading my Bible became a depressing thing for me to do so I stopped doing it. My prayers had not been answered like I thought they should have been, so I just stopped praying. I did not understand how

God could let these things happen to us so soon after we dedicated our lives to Him.

I mean what kind of God allows His children to suffer like that? What kind of God allows a fifteen-year-old to get addicted to crack cocaine? What kind of God allows a twenty-one-year-old boy with a two-year-old child to die in such a horrific accident? Surely not the God I loved and trusted. I was so mad.

I had prayed for Brian's healing, his deliverance from this addiction. I prayed for our family to be restored and for Kayla to have a daddy that could be a part of her everyday life as she grew up.

God took my brother away despite my prayers. He took him. Do you understand the magnitude of that? God betrayed me. Or least that was how I felt for a long time.

They say tragedy will either make you bitter or make you better. I was definitely bitter.

But you know what? God didn't give up on me even though He knew I blamed Him and was mad with Him. God patiently waited on me to come back to Him. He didn't reveal things to me all at once, but slowly I began to understand how God works.

Isn't it funny how God works sometimes? I was convicted to read the Bible in its entirety starting on the first day of my son's senior year of high school in 2014, and to finish it by the end of the school year. My intention was to make notes and highlight key Scriptures that would apply to my son's life during this important year of his life.

Remember now, I had not been reading my Bible for several years. This was going to be a stretch for me to read and study God's Word, because I had lost interest in His Word after feeling like He had ignored my prayers and abandoned my family.

But God is so amazing. He took my cold, broken, bitter heart and slowly transformed it as I studied His Word daily. He restored my faith as He revealed to me the many ways He answered my prayers for Brian and for our family. Because God knew what was about to take place in our lives, He saved my husband and convicted my heart to give my life to Him before we found out about my brother's addiction.

Why did He do this? I fully believe it was so He could carry us through the next few years. He knew we would need Him. He didn't want us to have to go through it without Him. My marriage probably would not have survived the stress of my family problems if my husband had not been a faithful servant of Jesus Christ. But because he had the love of Jesus in his heart, he had the patience of Job with my family.

God also revealed to me during my son's senior year of high school that Brian had indeed received complete and total healing, and he was no longer addicted to crack cocaine, or any other drug for that matter. God made sure that Brian had received Jesus in his heart before it was too late.

And get this … God used my father-in-law to do it. Do you see God's hand all over that? I wonder how I ever missed it. Brian's salvation experience happened just a few short weeks before he died.

God is never late. He is always right on time. He knew what was going to happen to Brian.

I now believe that God was with Brian every step of the way, and He knew Brian could not overcome his earthly struggles and be healed on this earth, so I truly believe, He made the necessary provisions to heal him eternally. Forever and ever.

My baby brother is whole, happy, and at the feet of Jesus today and forever. God never lost control of the situation. Yes, God could have waved His mighty hand and healed Brian on this earth. After all, God can do anything. But God wants us to submit to Him as willing vessels. He doesn't want puppets that He controls. His desire is that we come to Him willingly.

Did God answer my prayers? Yes. God healed my brother completely. God blessed our family with Brian's precious daughter, and she reminds me so much of her daddy. Kayla is beautiful, smart, and incredibly talented. She has recently discovered a love and talent for drawing and painting. A talent she no doubt got from her daddy. We have artwork all over our houses of pictures he drew and painted for us.

Kayla recently recreated a painting of a magnolia that her daddy painted years ago. A magnolia signifies stability and grace through the ever-changing ages. God is our stability and grace through the ever-changing ages and these paintings remind our family of that truth.

There will be times in our lives when we doubt God. We may even get mad and run from Him, but God will never leave us. He will always be patiently waiting for us to come back to Him.

As Romans 8:28 says, "And we know that in all things God works for the good of those who love Him, who have been called according to His purpose."

We all have a purpose from God. Even drug addicts are loved by God and can be used for His purposes. If you know someone that is struggling with addiction, whether a drug addiction or another addiction, please take a moment to lift them up in prayer. You will never know the torment they may be feeling. You may be the only person in the world praying for them. You may be the one person that is meant to lead them to Christ.

I am so thankful that God sent my father-in-law to my brother that night at the jail, and that today my brother is in the presence of our Lord and Savior. I look forward to the day when I can hug Brian's neck and tell him how much I love him and how very much I have missed him. But what I look forward to more than anything is falling at my Savior's feet thanking Him for never giving up on me. God is faithful.

JUST BREATHE

By Jessica Ingram

This isn't a story about how I struggled with anxiety, rediscovered God's peace, got better, and everything's been peachy since.

I still struggle with anxiety daily. I still have to rediscover God daily.

It all began for me in the sixth grade. In the fall of 2006, I started middle school. I moved from the colorful elementary school to a dismal tan building with "Rudd Middle School" rusting on the side.

I can't remember exactly when it started. I only have a few distinct memories from that time, but what I can remember still shocks and frightens me.

In the beginning I was pretty good at skipping school. I would claim I felt sick and even faked a fever so I wouldn't have to go to school. But my parents didn't fall for this long.

At first my parents believed that I was just being a typical "I don't wanna go to school" eleven-year-old. But it didn't take long for them to realize there was something much larger and unknown at play.

Some days, while sitting in the middle of class, I would be overcome by fear and anxiety. I would bolt out of the classroom, down the hall and into a stairwell. I would sit in a corner and scream and cry until Mrs. Shelnutt, a teacher and family friend that knew something was going on with me, came and got me. I would sit in the counselor's office or in her classroom until I calmed down or one of my parents came and got me.

Some days my parents would have to literally drag me out of the car kicking and screaming to get me to go in to school. My parents would have to leave me there in the office or the counselor's office. They didn't like leaving me behind in that state, but they didn't feel like they had much of a choice. They were like parents with a baby again. You just had to hand the crying child over to the caregiver and walk away knowing they were going to be okay.

After months of anxiety attacks, my parents sent me to see a Christian child counselor. I don't remember much of these visits either, but I still have my journal from that time. My counselor instructed me to write in the journal everytime I started to have anxiety. She told me to be specific about my fears when writing, to write down every detail about how I was feeling. Then she told me to write down one of the Bible verses she gave me about worry. I would write it over and over and recite it over and over.

Eventually, I got better. My last session with the counselor was in mid-February. I remember because I left my appointment and went straight to my birthday party.

No one could really tell me what happened to me that fall. Some think it was a severe case of the middle school jitters; some think I was under attack by Satan and his demons. Looking back now, I think it was probably a combination of the two.

I know it wasn't just middle school jitters because here I am, twenty-three years old and far away from my middle school days, and I still get the same heart-racing tightness in my chest on a daily basis.

I still struggle with anxiety, but I haven't had a severe anxiety attack since sixth grade. I haven't stopped suffering since sixth grade; I've just become better at hiding it. Not many people know that I struggle with anxiety, which I recognize is probably part of the problem. I'm not good at opening up about the things that I struggle with because — guess what? — I'm worried about what people would think of me. I get anxiety thinking about talking about my anxiety, so I just don't talk about it and I don't think about it. Even now as I type this, my heart is racing and my face is flushed.

It's been a long road trying to overcome my anxiety, and though I've made strides since the fall of 2006, I'm nowhere near where I want to be.

I want to be brave and fearless. I want to get on a boat or a train (surprisingly enough planes do not cause me anxiety) and not immediately feel my heart start racing as my mind imagines all the things that could go wrong.

I want to be able to spend time with my friends and family without worrying about what they think of what I look like, what I'm wearing, what I'm doing, or what I say. I'm tired of getting anxiety around my friends because I'm worried I'm not being fun enough or I'm being too weird or too clingy.

It takes a conscious effort on my part just to interact with people because I think it would be easier to sit at home and not have to deal with the anxiety that comes with going out. However, I also get anxiety when

I see friends hanging out and having fun without me. I get worried that they'll think that I'm not as fun as their other friends and they don't need me in their lives.

I always jump to the most extreme and worst conclusions. If someone doesn't text me back in a few hours, it's not that they were busy at work or just didn't look at their phone; it's that they are tired of me and don't want to talk to me and don't want to be my friend anymore. When my dentist instructed me to go see an oral surgeon about a bump in my mouth, I had decided that I had cancer before I even made it to the car.

I know that kind of thinking is toxic and all those fears are unfounded, but my conscious mind doesn't seem to communicate that to my subconscious very well.

Like I said at the beginning, I have to work daily to rediscover God and His peace. Some days it goes well. Some days it goes terribly.

I've found that worship music is my escape. I love music and nothing reminds me of God's power and love better than worship music. When I'm overcome with anxiety at work or in the car I will put on worship music and praise those fears away.

Don't misunderstand me. I would've never made it to where I am today without spending time praying and in God's Word, but there's just something about worship music that soothes me instantly. It's my love language with God.

I wish I had experienced a life without anxiety, but I know that I would not be the person I am today without it. It forces me to lean on the God who holds the universe on a daily basis. It has stretched and strengthened my faith in ways I didn't know were possible. I may not fully understand why I have to go through this until I reach the other side of eternity, but I know that my God is good and my God loves me and I can rest in that. It doesn't matter what people think of me, it doesn't matter what happens to me in this world, because I was made for a world infinitely better, where all my fears and anxieties will be wiped away.

This is my struggle, but it is all for God's glory.

GOD WILL NEVER LEAVE

By Tom Ingram

In 1939, Nazi Germany invaded Poland, and subsequently began World War II. In December 1941, the United States joined the war and changed my life forever. In January 1944, just months after turning eighteen, I was drafted and sent to Camp Blanding in Florida for training for the army. By the end of January 1945, I was in the middle of a war, watching my friends die around me, powerless to save them.

I was overseas a little more than three years and most of that time was spent in German-occupied Luxembourg. I was assigned to the 90th Infantry Division and 359th Infantry Regiment.

I was a machine gunner. I had to lie on my belly and put the stock on my shoulder. At nineteen years old, I was only twenty-two inches at the waist and the snow got as deep as twenty-one inches. The snow would hide me, and the Germans couldn't see me shooting at them.

We weren't prepared for the extreme cold and the snow. My feet were frostbitten. My toes turned black, and the medics wanted to cut my toes off. I eventually stopped going back to the aid station because they just wanted to cut my toes off.

The Germans shot a lot of American soldiers in the back, so we did the same thing. We didn't take many prisoners. We felt like we were justified in killing the Germans. If they could do it to us, we could do it to them.

I didn't really have a choice. If I didn't shoot them, they would've shot me. I had to get them first.

Most of my memories from that time come from the Battle of the Bulge in the Ardennes Forest. The Battle of the Bulge was fought from mid-December to late January. We lost a large number of soldiers and friends in that battle.

On January 31, 1945, I lost six of my buddies and five more were wounded.

My infantry was assigned the mission of capturing a small town in Germany and blocking the main road on the eastern outskirts of the town. Following a bitter fight, the company also secured houses on the western side of town.

During this fight, one of the officers was hit in the shoulder by sniper fire. As the rest of the infantry pulled back to secure protection, I remained with the officer, giving him first aid. The nearby medic refused to come help save him; he said it would be suicide. I ignored the continuous shots from tanks and machine guns as I dressed his wounds. I thought I could save him, but the wound was lower than I thought, and he went into shock. Unfortunately, the officer could not be saved, and I was forced to leave him. I was given a Bronze Star for trying to save my friend, John Dwyer.

Dwyer's wife is from Ireland, so when the war ended she decided to go back and visit her family. While over there, she decided it would be a good place to raise their two boys. One of the boys called me several years ago and wanted to know if I knew his dad. I told him I did. I told him I got a Bronze Star for trying to save him.

I told him if he wanted to go visit his dad's grave, I could take him. So we met in Luxembourg and went to the cemetery. I had visited the grave several times, so I led him to his father, and he was able to say his final goodbye.

All the soldiers killed in the Battle of the Bulge were buried just north of Bastogne, Belgium. When the war ended, the families were given four years to claim the bodies and have them shipped back to the U.S. for free. Today, that burial ground is just a pasture and the bodies that weren't claimed were dug up and buried in a military cemetery in Luxembourg.

It was hard to lose those friends. They were on my mind every day. I felt sorry for their families and loved ones back home. I did a lot of praying during those days. Both for me and for the families of the soldiers who had died.

I was also awarded a Purple Heart. The Purple Heart was given to me for being wounded in battle when a piece of shrapnel hit my leg.

Before I was drafted, I went to church every Sunday. My relationship with God was very real and strong. I've known the Lord my whole life, and I leaned on that a lot while at war.

Being away from home wasn't really a problem for me because I had been travelling alone since I was fourteen years old. It was hard thinking about my two brothers who were also off fighting the war. One was in the Pacific fighting and one was in the Air Force. Despite everything I went through, I would serve again in a heartbeat. I have pride that I was able to serve my country, and the friendships I built while overseas are irreplaceable.

The Lord was definitely with me through all of World War II. I can guarantee that. I faced four German tanks from forty yards away and lived to tell about it. I was never shot myself. I got one piece of shrapnel in my left leg, but that was it. The good Lord took care of me.

I am grateful to God that I came home from the war, but things haven't been easy. I've suffered from depression and post-traumatic stress disorder. I've been drawing disability since the day I was discharged because the frostbite and the hearing problems from the war have prevented me from working. I still go to therapy. I went through living hell. I lost friends; I took lives.

It's not easy to overcome the struggles of life, but for me, the key was to remember the almighty God is always with me. Go to church and surround yourself with Christian encouragers. Never forget to pray. The Lord will take care of you.

It may not be easy, but you should thank the Lord every day for your hardships. They are molding you into the person that God created you to be, and they should serve as reminders that God will never leave you.

GOD IS ALWAYS GOOD

By Vicky Jimmerson

About a year after my oldest son and his wife got married, they decided to start a family. After months with no success, my daughter-in-law went to the doctor. The doctor ran multiple tests and discovered she was not ovulating each month, so he put her on Clomid, a fertility drug, and eventually put her on the highest dose.

After months, still no pregnancy.

The doctor finally told them they would probably never be able to conceive naturally.

My son and daughter-in-law lived in Tuscaloosa at the time, and I was not with them when they received the news from the doctor. Though I knew their faith in God was strong, as is mine, I knew my son felt brokenhearted about possibly not being able to have their own children naturally.

They had a good support system with their church family in Aliceville and that helped them tremendously.

They came to our house to tell us the news and even brought an adoption application with them because they were going to look into it. When my son told me the doctor said they could not have children, I was crushed. Even though I knew I could love an adopted grandchild as much as my natural grandchild, this was my first, and I felt I was not getting the full grandparent roll.

We told them we would love that baby as much as if it were born into the family, but we also told them there is someone higher and more powerful than any doctor here on earth.

We advised them to pray and, of course, we would pray also. After a couple of months passed, my son called and told me my daughter-in-law was extremely sick, throwing up, and could not keep anything down.

He was asking my advice. Did I think he needed to take her to the doctor? It had not even crossed either of our minds that she might be pregnant. We had already accepted the fact that she could not get pregnant, and they had already started the application process for adoption. I told him yes, she didn't need to get dehydrated and she must have some kind of flu or stomach bug.

My son called me the next afternoon and told me he had taken her to the doctor and found out what was wrong with her.

When I asked him what was wrong, he said, "It's not something nine months won't cure." I immediately, of course, knew what he was talking about. I was in my car and had to stop, pull over and immediately say a prayer of thanksgiving for God's goodness and mercy and for answering our prayers.

I remember the first time I saw them after she found out about her pregnancy, how much they beamed with joy.

When she had our oldest granddaughter in Tuscaloosa, she said it was strange when the doctor came into her room with her file and she saw "infertile" written in big red letters on the front.

That was thirteen years ago and they now have three more beautiful daughters. She, sadly, has had a couple of miscarriages as well.

Every time I see those girls, I see four little miracles. Hearing them call me "Grandma" for the first time — it was so joyous. Words cannot describe that feeling.

God is always good, and He still performs miracles today just like He did when He walked on the earth. God is good, and He is always in control in every circumstance.

Sometimes our struggles come from our personal pain and suffering, and sometimes they come from watching our kids experience hardship. When I see my kids hurt, I hurt. If you have kids, you know exactly how that pain feels. I would do anything to take their pain away. However, I have learned I have to put it in God's hands.

I serve a big God. We were told there was no hope. We were told that she was infertile. You may be struggling with a situation right now. You may have even been told that there is no hope. However, I can tell you from experience that nothing is impossible for God. God is in control. Our story went from hopelessness to praise. I have seen Him work miracles. My oldest son and daughter-in-law have four girls to prove it.

SHAPE OF MY HEART

By Jan Johnson

My story begins on October 8, 2002. It was an ordinary weekday in our household. I woke the kids for school and got breakfast ready for them. I had just recently returned to work; I had been a stay-at-home mom for the previous five years when our third child was born. Now he was in Kindergarten, and I had started an office job at an insurance agency.

Our oldest son, Shaun, was sixteen years old and drove himself to school each day. This day Shaun's truck was in the shop, so he took his sister to school in my car.

We laughed and carried on that morning before everyone headed off to work and school.

The afternoon was not out of the ordinary either. My daughter was a cheerleader in middle school and had a game that night. She and I went to the game, leaving the guys at home.

Shaun asked to go to a different game with some friends and said he would be home after the game was over. It was just an average day in our lives – until it wasn't.

At eight o'clock that evening, my daughter brought me the phone. The woman on the other end told me our son had been involved in an accident, they were taking him to Andalusia Hospital, and I should meet them there.

I never had a thought that it was anything serious. I thought it was probably just a broken bone and we would return home shortly. I called some friends of the family to stay with our two other children while we were gone.

As my husband and I waited for the ambulance, I grew a little more anxious. It was taking an eternity for them to arrive. I asked the hospital staff for information, but they refused to tell me anything.

Finally, one ambulance arrived but it was carrying the other two friends. I asked about Shaun.

My answer came when the hospital chaplain arrived to take us to a private room. He told us our son had been killed in the accident.

On their way home, the brakes on the friend's truck failed. As the driver came to a stop sign, he geared the truck down to slow their speed. When he turned onto the paved road he lost control and the truck flipped. Our son died at the scene.

It didn't seem real or even possible that something like this could be happening. My entire body was shaking as we were driving home. When we arrived, cars were lined up and down our driveway and road. Our son's friends, family members, and neighbors were there to comfort us and take care of us.

The next days were a mix of emotions. I missed my son and everything that was taken from me with the end of his precious life. I felt so sorrowful for his young friends who had lost a classmate and close friend. Their sad faces streaming with tears was too much to bear. They were confused and dazed that such a terrible thing could happen to one of their own in this small town. They questioned, "Why would this happen to someone who was everybody's friend?"

My heart was broken for Shaun's good friend who was driving the truck. He had seen his best friend die, and nothing I could do or say would remove that memory from his mind. It seemed like more than any of us could endure.

What followed in the next days, weeks, and years are stories of God's grace and love for our family.

God used His people in our church, the community, and school to wrap our family in love and support. There are so many encouraging things that happened during this tragedy, and it is hard to choose which ones to tell. Without the prayer support of family and friends and the comfort of God, I don't know how or if our family would have survived this heartbreak.

The student body at the high school arranged prayer vigils. They had a special memorial service before the funeral, and they wrote poems to honor Shaun. One student wrote and recorded a song about him.

His football teammates considered it a privilege to be the pallbearers at his funeral.

An opposing football team even painted our son's number on their field at their homecoming game and had special prayer for us in honor of him.

The students made it a priority to be at events where my daughter cheered to support her, and they treated my youngest son as if he were their own little brother. Their love and support were felt throughout my daughter's high school years.

You may not remember what someone said or what they did, but you will never forget how they made you feel. The students made us feel loved and made it known that they loved our son.

I can remember times when I didn't know how I was going to get through the day, and in those moments God always sent someone to comfort me.

A friend would stop by with a word of encouragement and a hug. Or a group would drop off a meal for my family. Our mailbox was filled with cards daily. Sometimes I would see a friend of Shaun's and they would grace me with a memory they have of him.

You see, one of my greatest fears is that people will forget him. But God always provides a reminder for me, and the most important thing is that God has not forgotten him. My comfort and joy come in knowing that truth. In times of sorrow and distress I remind myself of God's promises:

" 'For I know the plans I have for you,' declares the Lord, 'Plans to prosper you and not to harm you, plans to give you hope and a future' " (Jeremiah 29:11).

As the years have passed, I have had to grieve many milestones of things my son never got to do here on this earth.

He missed prom, sports banquets, graduation ceremonies, and college adventures. As his classmates have aged, I've known of their marriages and the births of their children. But God is gracious, and He had already made a provision for me by blessing me with another son, who, surprisingly, looks like his older brother.

As Philippians 4:19 says, "And my God will meet all your needs according to the riches of His glory in Christ Jesus."

I will always have a hole in my heart in the shape of my firstborn.

But my God has given me peace, comfort, grace, and the knowledge that one day I will be reunited with him. I am grateful for the sixteen years God gave me with my son, and will always thank Him for the love and memories we shared.

1 Thessalonians 5:16–18 says, "Rejoice always, pray continually, give thanks in all circumstances; for this is God's will for your in Christ Jesus."

GOD WAS ALWAYS ON MY SIDE

By Tommy Jones

My parents and grandparents had me and my sister in church every time the doors were open. I gave my life to Jesus when I was eight years old at Royal Ambassadors camp at Shocco Springs in Talladega, Alabama. I have no doubt whatsoever that I was saved at eight, but I could see later in life that I didn't allow Jesus to be Lord of my life until January 13, 2006.

I grew up on a family farm in Alabama. My parents built a house next door to my grandparents. We were and are, still to this day, a tight knit family. I come from a very good family. We can count on each other. I am very thankful.

Even though I come from a good family and was in church all the time as a child, the enemy still had a plan of attack for my life.

When I was thirteen years old, I began looking at pornography and became addicted to it. My earliest memory of pornography was when I spent the night with one of my cousins and my cousin and I found my uncle's stash of pornographic movies. This was my first time seeing that type of junk. After seeing it for the first time, I began thinking about it a lot. At such an early age in life, I didn't understand what was going on within me nor the destruction that was growing within me. I remember having to feed this urge that was growing in me. As the junk began growing in me, I felt like I had to feed it. And whatever you feed will grow.

I would even checkout of school to come home and watch porn on the satellite while my parents were at work. At one point, I remember my parents and grandparents going to the garden to pick peas, and I turned the satellite on so I could watch the adult channels. I remember looking out the living room window to see if my family was coming back from the garden and then looking back at the television. I was living two lives. One I let everyone see, and one that I kept in secret.

I allowed the enemy to begin destruction in my life. I can look back now and see that was the enemy's plan all along. As John 10:10 says, "The thief comes only to steal and kill and destroy ..."

I learned that the enemy has a plan for our life, and it's called destruction. Through my high school years, the enemy used pornography to affect my perception of how women must really be.

I thought all women secretly wanted to be treated the way the women on the adult movies were treated. So, I began manipulating women to get what I wanted.

Sports began, and my pornography use slowed down some due to lack of time, but if I'm honest with myself, the pornography was still there, alive and well and still growing.

I became one of the more popular kids in high school, and between the popularity and the mindset I had about women, it was a recipe for disaster.

My late teen years and early twenties were a lot of the same, filled with one-night stands and many broken relationships. Around twenty-three years old, I married a young lady who was a great woman and still to this day is a great woman.

She is the mother of my two oldest children. We were married for seven years. Keep in mind that I still had not allowed Jesus to be Lord of my life yet, so I spent much of our marriage living two separate lives — one life that from the outside seemed great, and one secret life filled with pornography, adultery, and deceit.

Due to my work ethic, by the age of twenty-seven, I had climbed the corporate ladder to plant manager making over $100,000 a year at a local plastic plant.

Life was good for the most part. I had two wonderful kids, a loving wife, a nice house, a new SUV, a company truck, two cells phones, the works.

However, I still had this destruction living within me that had been growing for years and years. Between the clout that came with being the big dog at work, making good money, and the destruction growing inside my heart, there came the temptation for adultery, and I took the bait, hook, line, and sinker.

I can attest that a covenant between a husband and a wife is real. I have never felt anything like what I felt when I committed adultery for the first time. Something spiritual happened. Some of it was conviction, and some was condemnation.

Conviction says, "Come on now, you can do better. You know what you are doing is wrong and you need to repent."

Condemnation says, "You idiot, you know better than that, now just look at you. No matter what you do you will never be whole again." The enemy is the father of lies, which is where condemnation comes from.

But I didn't realize this until later down the road.

I began believing the lies of the enemy, and my mindset was that it didn't really matter what I did, because I had already done too much bad stuff. So, I tried to cover this up in my mind with the fact that I was the big dog at work; I made more money than all my friends; I was the shot caller — I was the man. Insecurities masked by pride began leading my path.

I decided it would be best to divorce my wife so I could be with the woman I was cheating on her with. I actually married this woman and we stayed married for eight months. In all honesty, my new wife was amidst a tough time in her life as well.

Pride was leading the way, and no one could tell me anything.

At this point, I was not listening to anyone, and I was in the worst turmoil of my entire life. I felt alone, scared, worthless, untrustworthy, and like a joke. I began looking for things to help me cope with the fact that I had split my family up through divorce, and the enemy was in my ear every second of the day. I began going to the gym twice, sometimes three times, a day and began using steroids to try and get the outside cleaned up, although my inside was still a mess. Isn't that what we do a lot? We try and clean the outside up instead of getting the inside cleaned up first.

Well, I finally got the outside looking the way I thought I needed to look, and guess what? It still didn't deliver me from the turmoil I was experiencing. After steroids, I figured I could try other drugs to help me cope with all the destruction in my life.

I smoked weed, and it didn't stop the hurt. I used pills, but they didn't stop the hurt. Cocaine stopped the hurt for a little while, but pretty soon it stopped working too. I used meth, and it worked for a little while, but it didn't stop the hurt forever. More women didn't stop the hurt.

At that point in my life, getting and using drugs had taken the place of my family and my career. Before I knew it, I had spiraled down from being married with kids at home and a successful career, to divorced, unemployed, and bankrupt. I found myself with no college education, unemployed, paying child support and bills, and divorced for the second time. I was at rock bottom.

I look back now and can see where God was sending me help all throughout my journey, and in the middle of all that mess, God sent me my wife today — twelve years and still running strong. I think I love her more every day that passes because she saw me in the absolute worst time of my life, loved me, and stuck by my side.

After being on a three-day drug binge, I came home and my wife, my dad, and three good friends were sitting in my trailer and extended tough love to me. They told me I had to get help.

I told them the next day that I would let them take me to rehab. I checked in rehab on January 11, 2006, and on January 13, I called my wife and my dad and asked both of them to come get me.

I told them, "I'm not like these people up here. I don't need rehab." They both told me that they loved me and that they were not coming to get me because they really did love me.

The night of January 15, I was scared, alone, brokenhearted, defeated, and humiliated, and I said to God from my knees in the rehab room, "God, I don't know if you are real or not but if you don't help me, I'm going to end my life."

As I woke up sometime later that night on the floor of the room, I noticed a presence standing in front of me. I couldn't make out the face but just knew it was good. It reached its hand down to me and lifted me up, and for the first time in twenty-one years, I didn't hear the enemy's voice.

I said, "I don't know who You are, but I will serve You from now on." I know now that it was Jesus or the Holy Spirit or God who came to me that night. He had all power, and when He came, the enemy left.

I spent ten more days in rehab learning tools to use to continue to live without drugs and hurt when I got back home.

My wife was still in college at the time, and I can remember her sitting in the waiting room of the outpatient clinic I was going to five days a week for six months doing her homework. She drove me every day, sat and waited on the meeting to finish, and then would drive me back home.

During the three months of being unemployed, I read the Bible. I read it because I had to know more about the Jesus who delivered me. I started in the Old Testament and couldn't understand it, so I jumped over to the New Testament.

I remember after I finished reading the Bible, I told God, "It looks to me like most of the people were a bunch of knuckleheads, and You chose to use them. Heck, I qualify as a knucklehead, so I see that You can use me too." God doesn't call the qualified, He qualifies the called. You can be used by God.

My wife, all of our children, and extended family began going to church and began learning more and more about the power and love of

God. We couldn't get enough of God. We have seen His amazing love and power firsthand.

I look back over my life, and I can see the main thing the enemy was after was my identity, and the thing God gave me was my identity in Him. I see now that I am a child of God, and I am learning through Scripture, prayer, counsel, and worship who I am because of who He is. I can honestly tell you that I never feel alone anymore, and I know that God is always in my corner. Because I made Jesus the Lord over my life, He has blessed me with a happy marriage, children who are saved and love the Lord, the best career I've ever had, and I get to work in ministry from time to time now. Not too bad for a knucklehead with God on his side. Thank you, Jesus!

FLOOD OF 1990

By Jane Lambert

What started off as a regular day quickly turned into a nightmare. But first, let me backup and give you a little history.

In May 1989, I moved my family from Mobile, Alabama to Eufaula, Alabama where I had taken a job at the Eufaula Adolescent Center. Soon after, I married my second husband and moved to Jack, Alabama. Since we were in a single-wide, two-bedroom trailer at that time, we placed all my furniture and life belongings into a storage unit in the nearby city of Elba.

The morning of March 16, 1990, my husband, a neighbor, our three-week-old son, and myself loaded up and took a trailer to Elba to move my stuff to our new home. We started loading stuff up from the storage unit. We laughed and joked all morning as the baby slept. We had loaded a television, ironing board, and a few other things when it started to rain. Since my husband had to report to work at the prison at 2 p.m., we decided we would quit for the day, get something to eat, and come back the next morning.

It was a typical rainy day. It had rained off and on the previous few days so no one thought there was cause to be alarmed.

Later that evening, after my husband, Kieff, had gone to work, our neighbor, Mr. Larry, came over and brought me a flashlight and told me the weather might get bad. I still thought it would probably just be another thunderstorm.

A few hours later, Mr. Larry came back and said it looked like Elba was going to flood. His wife had gone to Elba to help her parents get some things out of their house and moved before the flooding started.

Now being from Mobile, rain, storms, and hurricanes were nothing new, but flooding … I had never experienced that.

Shortly after Mr. Larry left the second time, the power went off.

Lord help me, there I was in the middle of the woods, no street lights, with a three-week-old baby and no way to warm a bottle. Now I was beginning to get a little anxious. I thought if only Kieff were home things would be better.

The rain continued to come. I knew Kieff should have been home by midnight, but it was getting close to 2 a.m. We had no cell phones so there was no way to call. I couldn't even call Mr. Larry.

It wasn't much later that Kieff came in and I thought, "Okay, everything will be alright now." He told me it looked like the levee wasn't going to hold and Elba was going to flood.

But this meant nothing to me — I didn't understand the implications. I just wanted to get up the next morning and finish getting my belongings and the kids' clothes and toys so we could bring them home and get settled.

The next morning we awoke to the worst. The city of Elba was completely under water. People were without homes, power, and water, but I still could not comprehend the devastation that had taken place. The city was under water for four days. We weren't allowed to even go into town to check on my storage unit.

Once we were allowed to return to Elba, it was unbelievable. Who would have ever thought water could do such damage? The smell was terrible. It was hot and humid. The people were just lost.

We were lucky our home wasn't destroyed like so many, but it did destroy everything I had worked for all my life: my children's toys, clothes, and many things dear to their hearts.

Several years prior to my marriage to my current husband, I was married to the father of my two oldest children. At the age of twenty-seven he was diagnosed with Immunoblastic Sarcoma and given a short time to live. It was a long, tough battle. He lived eighteen months and died at the age of twenty-nine. Our children were seven and four at the time.

Three years later, their grandfather shot and killed their grandmother and then killed himself. Needless to say, the years between 1982 and 1987 were some tough ones for the kids and myself. Many memories and keepsakes that I had kept for them were in this storage unit.

The storage unit was packed tight from top to bottom, front to back. When we finished filling it up, there wasn't even room for the Christmas wrapping paper my mom and I had bought on sale after Christmas. I thought things would probably be okay since there wasn't much room for things to move around in there. Boy, was I wrong.

When Kieff opened the unit, it was heartbreaking. The water had rushed through with such force that even my piano was crushed. There was a terrible stench. The rocking chair my first husband bought for our firstborn son was broken; my daughter had numerous Cabbage Patch dolls and Precious Moments dolls from her childhood, and now they were all covered in red mud and had a terrible odor.

You had to be careful to watch for rats and snakes. They told us anything plastic could not be kept because of the possibility of disease. As fast as we were cleaning out and putting the unsalvageable stuff out by the road for trash pickup, others were rummaging through the pile taking what they wanted.

I had a lot of depression glass passed down by the children's great-grandmother, and all of it was broken by the force of the water.

A box of jewelry I saved for my daughter that her father had given me was nowhere to be found. My son was a big Star Wars fan, and he had every Star Wars toy there was, but not anymore.

I was able to find the Bible given to us when their father died, but it was covered in mud. I still have it to this day. My high school diploma and my diploma from nursing school were covered in red mud, but I still have them, mud and all.

Tears flowed and anger came. I couldn't understand how all this was fair. I had worked so hard for many years with nothing to show now. I lost a husband at a very young age, and I had been a single mother working two, sometimes three, jobs to provide for myself and the children.

"How could this one storm have taken everything away from me?" I wept.

I felt so sorry for my children. Everything that was a part of their childhood, that was a part of their life with their father, and a part of our home was gone. They hadn't even had time to adjust to moving and leaving their friends and family and now this. I was angry. How could God continue to take away from me?

It took a few days for it to sink in that we really were blessed. I had my life, my children, a new baby, my husband and, most importantly, a roof over my head. Many people could not say that at that time. They didn't just lose stuff stored in a building; they lost their homes, their jobs, their businesses. There was devastation all across the little town of Elba, Alabama.

So many times I felt overwhelmed, like the weight on my shoulders was overloaded. Truth be told, God was walking every step with me. I lost some material things. Yes, they were important; they meant something to us. I felt like a failure as a mother. I had moved my children promising them things would be better and then this happened. But we all still had each other.

I think of that flood every time I go to town. I think of the things I had in that building that I loved — like my red boots. I loved those boots. I never bought another pair of red boots.

A flood in a little town called Elba. Home to less than 4,500 people. Water rose fifty feet and rushed through that little town destroying everything in its path. I was familiar with hurricanes — I had lived through hurricanes Camille and Frederic — but not a flood that took everything. Today I am thankful that I still have the most important thing in life: my family. God is so good.

Most important was that even in the darkest times, God never left me. There is a gospel song about times when we are on the mountain and times when we are in the valley. It says without trials we might forget to pray. Isn't that so true?

So many times we don't really pray until we need something from God. The light will come, this is not our forever home.

I remind myself and others frequently of that fact, and that God did not promise us a perfect life — a life without loss, pain, or sorrow.

What He did promise us is that He would always be with us, and that with Him we will have a forever home without tears and sadness.

Life is all about trials and temptations, and I have had my share. But each day I thank God that He did not let me give up or give in. He lifted my eyes to see Him and not the world.

WHAT AN AWESOME GOD

By Karen Raines Layton

In March 1986, I married my high school sweetheart. Life was good. I had no idea at that time of the challenges and heartbreak that lay ahead for me.

I have always loved children and felt a call to teach, so I made that my vocation.

When my husband and I decided it was time to have children, God had a different time frame in mind.

I thought His timing was to teach me to trust Him with one of the most important goals in my life: having children. Those lessons in trust and faith took five years. Thankfully, they shaped and molded me for my future.

After two years of trying to pray hard enough to get God to do what I wanted in regards to children, I finally let go.

God helped me get to the point where I understood and readily accepted that He knew best, and if He didn't want me to have children then I was okay with that.

After three more years of infertility we found out I was pregnant. Mike and I already had a trip planned to Disney World when we found out the wonderful news.

My doctor suggested that we not go because I would lose the baby. She did not just advise against going in case I lose the baby.

She said with certainty, "You will lose this baby."

She knew some things that we did not know regarding the pregnancy. She assumed I would not want to be far from home when I suffered the likely miscarriage. But God had other plans.

We did not lose the baby.

I went into labor at twenty-eight weeks, but, once again, God had other plans for Ashton and she would not be born that early. He used good doctors, nurses and medicine to carry out His will for this baby.

I was bedridden for ten weeks with a pump giving me medicine to stop the labor. It worked, Ashton was born a healthy baby at thirty-eight weeks.

My next pregnancy was an ectopic pregnancy. I lost that baby in July 1994. The series of events during that loss could have kept me from ever having any more children but again, God had other plans. The decisions that He led us to make during the ectopic pregnancy made my third pregnancy possible.

On Thursday, January 26, 1995, we found out I was pregnant again. Needless to say, Mike and I were thrilled. But two days later, my husband was killed in an automobile accident.

Had I not learned to completely trust God during my season of infertility, I would not have survived Mike's death. My world was devastated. Ashton had just turned two years old, I was pregnant, and I lost my husband.

I can honestly say that I had some long discussions with God about losing the love of my life and having to raise our children alone. I so wanted God to tell me the where, when and how my life was going to work out now.

He very sweetly told me to trust Him just one day at a time. I told Him that was not the way I wanted it. But now I am so grateful I did not get my way.

Learning to trust Him one day at a time, sometimes one hour to the next, has been some of the sweetest experiences I have ever had. My faith and knowledge of who God is has dramatically changed.

James 1:2–4 says, "Consider it pure joy, my brothers and sisters, whenever you face trials of many kinds, because you know that the testing of your faith produces perseverance. Let perseverance finish its work so that you may be mature and complete, not lacking anything."

I am so grateful that my time with God during my infertility season taught me how to truly trust God. I was confident that Ashton, the new baby and I would be okay. Losing Mike was definitely not in my plans, but I knew we would be okay trusting God one day at a time. God taught me what I think He wants us all to know: that we can and need to trust Him everyday, hour by hour, even minute by minute.

Trusting Him like that does not mean grief or heartache won't be there — it will — but He very lovingly carries our burdens even when we have no idea that He is.

Grief is a part of healing, but there were times when the grief was suffocating. There were also times when I would wallow in complete misery. I would wallow two to three days at a time.

99

I finally realized that Satan wanted me to do that. I also realized all I had to do was ask for God's help to get me out of my pity party and sadness, and He would.

I usually saved my grieving until the wee hours of the night when Ashton was asleep so I wouldn't make her sad too.

My last night like that was one of my sweetest moments with God. It was late at night and the grief was absolutely overwhelming. I told God that I just couldn't stand the grief anymore. I asked Him to take it from me. I did not have a blanket around my shoulders, but it felt as though a physical blanket of grief was lifted from my body. It is an experience that I will always cherish. God is so sweet and loving to take our deepest sorrows and hurts. We just need to turn it all over to Him.

I knew shortly after Mike died that the baby I was carrying was a boy. God completely took care of the pre-labor problems that I had before even though the same medical issues still existed for me. I had no problems with the pregnancy and Michael Perryman Raines, Jr. was born healthy at thirty-eight weeks.

My relationship with God has changed. I know now if everything and everyone were taken away from me, but I still had God, then I would be okay. Mind you, I am not saying I would be happy if that happened, but I know now I would be okay. I have learned to find my joy in Christ, not in people and things around me.

People and things are temporary and can be gone in a minute, but nobody can take God from me. My relationship with Him has become so sweet.

My favorite Scripture now is Romans 8:28, which says, "And we know that in all things God works for the good of those who love Him, who have been called according to His purpose."

God brings some type of good out of every situation for those who love Him and are following Him. I have seen that good happen over and over again in many different scenarios. Sometimes you may have to ask God to help you see the good.

Almost six years after Mike's death, God blessed me with an amazing man to be my husband and a father to my children. He brought along two children of his own and then God gave us two surprise blessings together! We now have his two, my two, and our two. We're almost the Brady Bunch.

My life has been very full and blessed even when the blessings weren't recognizable at the time. The greatest blessings in my life have come from fully surrendering to Christ.

Getting knocked to my knees and having to daily depend on God has been amazing. Getting to know such a loving, compassionate God has forever changed me.

Whatever God wants to happen or allows to happen can be used for His glory and my good.

Proverbs 3:5–6 instructs us to "trust in the Lord with all your heart and lean not on your own understanding; in all your ways submit to Him, and He will make your paths straight."

We serve an awesome God who graciously serves us. I consistently pray now that I see things and people through His eyes so I can learn more and serve Him in the best way possible. I am very thankful for all that God has done for me and my family, and for what He has taught me. Whatever you are going through, turn it over to Him, then count on His gracious and loving hands to guide you through it. Understand that He is working for your good whether it looks like that or not. It will be an amazing walk.

THANKS BE TO GOD

By Todd Ledford

My name is Todd Ledford, and I am a grateful recovering addict. My clean and sober date is November 7, 2008.

I was born in Ozark, Alabama, and lived a typical southern boy's life: baseball, football, and the outdoors. My parents divorced when I was five years old, and at my young age, I don't recall it being all that traumatic. At least not at that time. Life rocked on like this for several years, but at the age of eleven, my mom remarried and moved this funny-talking Southern boy to Southern California. I recall *this* as one of the most traumatic events in my life.

It created a whole new level of fear and anxiety in me that fueled my insecurities and need for acceptance. I was shy and insecure, and being the focus of all the other kids' negative attention was overwhelming.

Because of my stepdad's career we moved around a lot. I didn't realize how much until I was asked to do a timeline of my life. I discovered that we moved seven times in five years, and I changed schools a total of six times. I can still remember those anxious feelings. The physical stress of walking into a new classroom or stepping onto a playground was almost debilitating.

It was always easier to fit in with the fringe crowd. You know, the ones everyone considers the troublemakers. Not that I got into a lot of trouble, but the opportunity for drinking and partying was a common occurrence.

I was first introduced to alcohol and marijuana at the age of fourteen. I never really liked the way alcohol made me feel. I never liked getting drunk and sick. But marijuana was a different story.

Marijuana became my drug of choice, and it wasn't long before it became a daily routine. I even started selling it. Not really for the money, but to help pay for my own personal use. Plus, it was easy to get people to hang around with you and party if you had dope.

It wasn't long before marijuana wasn't enough and other drugs entered the picture. I began experimenting with cocaine, meth, pills, and almost any drug around. But looking back, it was always marijuana and alcohol that were my main drugs.

At the age of twenty-one, I moved back to Alabama, finished college, and received my bachelor's degree in business administration. I found a position in the medical field, and despite having a successful career, alcohol and drugs were still very prominent in my life.

Working in the medical field in the early 1990s, I saw large amounts of narcotic pain medication pouring into medical practices. Working as office manager, it was not uncommon to see drug representatives wheel boxes of Xanax, Lortab, and other narcotics into offices.

This is where the game started to change for me. I began experimenting with narcotic pain medicines, and due to chronic back pain, I was able to get prescription narcotics very easily.

Pain pills became my new drug of choice. They gave me a different kind of euphoria. They made everything feel okay. I had no worries or stress, and I seemed to be able to function at a higher level. I was able to talk with people, and for the first time in a long time, I felt comfortable in my own skin. Pain pills did for me what I could not do for myself.

My career was booming. I was making a lot of money and met a wonderful woman. We got married and started a family. From the outside looking in, our lives looked picture perfect. The BMW was in the driveway, and we were very active in our church. I was even serving as the church treasurer. But life on the inside was beginning to take its toll.

I knew the pills were becoming a problem, and I was going to great lengths to get more. I was looking in people's medicine cabinets, and manipulating and stealing meds from family and friends. It was taking more and more to achieve the same high, and the pills had become the first thing I thought of in the morning and the last thing I thought of at night.

I knew I needed to stop and would muster up the resolve to stop for several days or even weeks. But the withdrawals were getting worse and worse, and I was drawn back in time and time again.

Just when I thought I had things under control, I would be presented with another opportunity, and I would be off to the races once again.

I didn't want anyone to know I had a problem, but I began crying out to God and begging for help. I didn't know where else to turn. I did what the church tells us we are supposed to do and took it to the altar. The problem was that when I left church I didn't know what to do next.

I finally decided to confide in a friend. He and his wife came to my house and prayed over me and anointed me with oils, but it still wasn't getting any easier.

It was around this time that I started to sense something in my spirit. I felt like God was speaking to me. I kept hearing these same words over and over again: "I gave you My life, why can't you give Me twenty-eight days."

Well, I knew what that meant, and I didn't want to do it. I knew He was asking me to go to treatment. But if I did that then everyone would know I was not perfect. They would know all this was just a lie, and I was really just a drug addict.

So for two years, I continued in the struggle, the lies, the stealing, the manipulation. It got to the point that the drugs and alcohol were no longer working. I could no longer capture the ease and comfort I once did. It was at that moment I knew I was in trouble, and I seriously considered going to my house, laying out that old blue tarp and putting a bullet in my mouth. But I knew my boys would be the ones to find me, and I could not bear that.

It wasn't long before one of the physicians walked into my office and asked me if I was okay.

I said, "No, I need help." I was sick and tired of being sick and tired.

So on October 28, 2008, my wife delivered me to a drug and alcohol treatment center north of Birmingham. It was one of the worst days of my life, but there was also some sense of relief.

I tell people all the time, I didn't go to treatment to find God, twelve steps, Narcotics Anonymous, or Alcoholics Anonymous. I just wanted some help.

I was told very early on that drugs and alcohol were not my problem. They were just a symptom of my problem. They explained that I had a spiritual malady that could only be relieved by a conscious contact with God. And I needed to work these twelve steps as a process of discovering why I used drugs and alcohol.

It was about this time that I became teachable. I began listening to what they were saying, and applying some of the simple suggestions: prayer, meditation, and journaling.

I remember very vividly one particular morning when I awoke very early and began my daily routine. I was treating them like a checklist of tasks because my goal was to get to the gym before another guy and beat him to the treadmill.

I recall rushing into the kitchen for a cup of coffee, and as I was walking out of the kitchen, a little voice in my head whispered, "Slow down, slow down." So I slowed my pace and walked over to the fireplace and sat on the hearth.

I had this overwhelming need to pray. I still don't remember what that prayer was, but what I do remember is that I was no longer in that room alone.

I was in the presence of Christ, and from a spiritual perspective I felt and sensed that He reached over, caressed me on the head, and said, "It's okay, it's okay."

It was one of the most amazing experiences I have ever had in my life. I wish I could convey it more adequately, and I'm sure it will be hard for some to believe. But we all have a story about our encounters with Christ.

This is what changed my life. It confirmed for me that what the Bible says is true. I also believe the reason that I was not healed at the altar or on my living room floor, when I was being prayed over and my head anointed with oil, was because God wanted me in a recovery program. A program where one of the fundamental principles is that I can't keep what I have unless I'm willing to give it away.

I've been clean and sober for over nine years now, and it has absolutely nothing to do with me. My best thinking got me into a mess, and the only thing that has saved me is the grace, love, and mercy of Jesus Christ.

I've also come to believe in the sovereignty of God and the timing of God. And I believe someone will read this that needs to know there is hope. Whether it's drugs, alcohol, pornography, nicotine, or something else, God is still in the miracle business and there is help from heaven.

I'm reminded of what someone once told me, "God didn't open the gates of heaven and let me in. He opened the gates of hell and let me out."

Thanks be to God.

WHY, GOD?

By Lexie Lee

My name is Lexie and I am twenty-three years old.

About a year ago a lifelong friend of mine asked, "After all of the things that have happened to you, how do you still believe there is a God? Why does God let such awful things happen to good people?" Here lies a glimpse of my story — it does not define me, but it does define Him.

Anyone that knows me would probably describe me as a soft-spoken little lady most often seen hugging a dog, playing with kids, gawking at a good sunset, or attempting to bake something to satisfy my sweet tooth.

Growing up, I was the more reserved, think-before-you-speak, helping-hand kind of little girl. Despite the God-questioning adversities I have been put through, I can still say that is who I am today.

I was raised in what I thought was a normal home with my wonderful, hard-working mother, a stern, strict father, my half-sister who was older by five years, and a sister who was younger by two years.

Unfortunately, I cannot say that Jesus Christ was the center of our household. We went to the Baptist church in town consistently for about a year when I was in the first grade. This is where I learned about the Man that I said my bedtime prayers to every night, my constant, ultimate Father.

Being so young, I could not even begin to wrap my head around the story of the gospel. Jesus died for *me*? Jesus loves *me*? I don't even know Him!

After learning about Him in Sunday School and after two Vacation Bible Schools, I made the biggest and most important decision of my life. I accepted Jesus into my heart and was baptized at a very young age.

I have always had a lot of admiration for my mother. She was the unplanned, youngest of five, and began working at fourteen years old.

Growing up, aunts and uncles were always telling my sisters and me stories about our mom.

She was a free-spirit, selfless, and had a smile and red hair that brought all the boys to their knees. She was constantly working so she could support herself and our family. Waitressing, cleaning houses, bartending, you name it. Anything to make sure she was putting food on the table for her family. She did this single-handedly as she tried to shield my sisters and me from my father's own monster — addiction.

My father truly began as a good one. He was a man who provided for his family, coached ball teams, and wanted only the best for his daughters.

Although he was a strict, slave-driving, and self-seeking man who most certainly believed in discipline and spankings, my heart could never believe anything less than he was my dad and he hung the moon.

As I grew up, my naivety slowly but surely started to fade. The minute my older half-sister could legally choose to live with her biological father, she left our family to live across the state. From then on, I noticed the tensions in my house. My father began to check out not only mentally, but physically for days at a time.

My mom would get off of work at her job waitressing, gather my younger sister and me, and drive from hotel to hotel until she found him hiding out.

I have vague memories watching from the car window as my father opened hotel doors looking like he hadn't slept in days. My mom and dad were constantly fighting. Arguments about my father's absenteeism at home, at church, at school functions, and softball games started to become more violent as my father proved himself to be manipulative and verbally abusive.

As a little girl, I wondered why God allowed these to be my parents' circumstances. There were times when I would pray they were not even married. I knew my mother deserved better. She deserved the world.

It was then that I began to realize my mother was overcompensating to make up for my father's lack of support.

On his pay days, my father wouldn't bring any money home because he spent every dollar to satisfy his drug fix.

All the while, my younger sister and I were expected to come home with A honor roll report cards and to excel in softball with no questions asked.

My first week of high school started with a bang when one morning, Momma woke me up to tell me that my father's luck had run out.

After my father was on one of his week-long missing highs, he was arrested and sentenced to twenty years in prison on two felony counts of distribution of meth and possession of cocaine.

My mother held both of her crying daughters apologizing for him that morning before school. She promised to be for us what he wasn't and assured us we were on our way to living a much better life without him.

We prayed together for the first time in a long time. I again questioned the Lord. Why was this happening to us?

Trying to live life as normally as possible after Dad's arrest was the new objective for our little family.

I knew that my dad's arrest was the talk of town. Deep down I felt like people were naturally expecting my sister and me to fall into the wrong crowd and follow in our dad's footsteps. I was determined not to let that happen. After all, my mother raised me better than that.

The following year, one morning my mom walked out of the bathroom after showering, holding her face in her hands. This was the first time I had seen her cry since my dad was arrested.

I followed behind her into her bedroom where she asked me to feel the lump on her breast. She admitted that she had been feeling this lump in her breast for a couple of months, and she was so scared of what it could be. She was *scared*. A word I had never heard my momma say. *Scared.*

Several doctor's appointments, a PET scan, a mammogram, and biopsy later, it was confirmed that my best friend and mother had stage 4 breast cancer. Now really, why God?

My mom knew she had to fight it because she was all that my sister and I had. She agreed with her doctors to complete vigorous rounds of chemotherapy and radiation. The chemotherapy she was taking was Adriamycin, also called "the red devil." It proved to be a form of the devil himself.

I remember being fifteen years old and driving my mom to and from her chemo and radiation appointments. I first saw and understood what strength was as I walked with her through this journey. My mom lost so many things — her hair, her breast, her pride, and her confidence. However, the strength that woman had was immeasurable and that was something she never lost.

Sick as could be, she never missed a softball game for me and my sister. Bald as could be, she never lost her hope for tomorrow and her hope for remission. In between the nauseating days spent moving from the toilet back to her bed, she would clean houses during the day and bartend at night. She still put her faith in the Lord and trusted that He would get her through this valley.

One thing I will never forget is the team of people we had behind us that made everyday possible. Friends, family, teammates, coaches, coworkers, and teachers surrounded us with love when we needed it the most, casseroles and meals when no one had the time or money to get food, and donations that kept our family's finances afloat.

By the Lord's merciful grace, my mom was still joking around, smiling the most perfect smile, and cheering up everyone around her. She was definitely the medical staff's favorite patient, and even the patients' favorite patient.

Needless to say, Momma was a pillar of strength for all to see. The nurses who cared for and loved her were the people who inspired me to become a nurse. A far-off goal I was sure I would never accomplish. No matter how sick my mom was, she was always stern with two pieces of advice:

1. Never give up on your dreams
2. Never settle for less than what you deserve — happiness.

Taking her first piece of advice, along with a little push from her, I began college and went for my bachelor's of science degree in nursing.

Throughout every year in school I managed to stay on top of my grades and juggle two jobs. I was a lifeguard, a resident assistant in the dorms, a waitress, and a bartender during college. I was willing to do anything to stay in school, pay my bills, and send my mom extra cash to help her get by — although she refused to take it. I promised to make her proud and be the first one in our family to earn a college degree.

When it came to nursing school, I didn't truly know what I was signing up for. The homework, studying, validations, clinical rotations, and exams were just about more than I could handle.

My first semester of nursing school was three weeks shy of being over. I had final exams and one more clinical left to go when I received the most traumatizing news of my life. I had just pulled into the nursing building parking lot to turn in hard copies of clinical care plans when my cancer-fighting, hardworking, and loving mother called.

"Hey baby, it's your momma. Do you have a second? Because I'm sitting up here at the doctor's office. It is back and stronger than before. They are thinking months."

Everything around me went black, and I was completely numb, crying out to God in my car. Now really, why God?

Four years of battling this monster and two remissions were enough for her. The doctors had given her the maximum amount of chemotherapy and radiation they had to offer. The only thing they could offer her now was advice to go spend the rest of her time at home surrounded by loved ones. After all she had been through, she deserved her last months to be as happy and as comfortable as possible, free of doctor's appointments and emergency room visits.

Too soon hospice was called, and what was originally thought to be months turned into just a few short weeks. I lost my best friend and mother a week before Thanksgiving at twenty-one years old.

So my friend asked me at twenty-two years old, "After all of the things that have happened to you, how do you still believe there is a God? Why does God let such awful things happen to good people?" This was honestly a hard question for me to answer immediately.

I paused for a long time before answering her. All throughout my life, I questioned God and asked Him why. Why me? Really, God? What else?

I answered her when it finally hit me. I still believe there is a God because during the downpours of sadness and struggles He allowed me to go through, He was there the entire time, right next to me.

Jesus followed up in ways I never thought He would. Jesus showed Himself through the people that poured love onto me and my family throughout this journey. Jesus showed Himself through my momma when my father got locked away and throughout her fight with cancer. Jesus showed Himself through the friends, neighbors, family, strangers, and every person who helped and prayed for our family while Momma was sick as can be. Jesus showed Himself through all of the doctors, nurses, receptionists, and technicians that showed my mother love and showed kindness to her daughters.

Jesus showed Himself through my high school and college friends who encouraged me and prayed over me without hesitation. Jesus showed Himself when my entire family gathered around my mom on her last day as we prayed and sang "Amazing Grace" just before her last breath.

Jesus then showed Himself when He gave my baby sister strength to pull herself out of an abusive relationship and deliver life to my perfect nephew just two years later.

Jesus showed Himself by placing a relationship in my life that brought me so much love, laughter, and encouragement in Christ.

Most recently, Jesus showed Himself by allowing me to graduate as a nurse and work alongside brilliant doctors and nurses for one of the nation's highest ranked pediatric hospitals.

If all of these people and examples of love do not prove He is at work, then I am not sure what does. All of these people were the hands and feet of Christ, which is exactly what God wants His people to be.

My prayer used to be, "Jesus, can You please make this hurt stop? Can You please stop making bad things happen to good people?"

Now I stand firm in this prayer: "Jesus, can You change me and hold my heart to be able to handle what I am going through?" My story proves that God can and He will.

Jesus will pour into your life through the relationships that you build with one another. This short, earthly life is about showing one another kindness, mercy, forgiveness, and love through Him.

We have to stop believing that the Lord takes, and realize that He instead gives. He teaches appreciation, love, honor, patience, and grace. We just have to be still enough to listen and recognize these blessings amongst troublesome times.

Today, I continue to fall short as a Christian. I am deeply flawed and forget to talk to God sometimes. I do not have a perfect attendance record in church, and every now and then I let a cuss word fly.

Still today, I find myself asking, "Why God?" when I see innocent children with debilitating illnesses, when going through a breakup, and when my bank account only has $2.38 left until my next paycheck.

In this flawed world, we will continue to run into disappointments and struggle. Why? Because Earth is not heaven. How incredible is it to know that there is a place that is perfect with no addictions, no sickness, no hate, no heartbreak, no judgment, and no disappointment? The Lord is shaping each of our lives with times of joy and struggle so that we may glorify Him.

A GOOD, GOOD FATHER

By Zane Sanders Mahone

I have always eaten healthy. I was always athletic and fit. I was a dancer, gymnast, soccer player, and I cheered at Auburn University, so you'd think I would have an easy time staying fit and looking my best. You'd think I would find a balance after I graduated college. You'd think I would've known how to work out and stay fit. I should have it all together.

Unfortunately, staying fit, healthy, and happy was nearly impossible after I graduated from Auburn University in 2016. I was married three weeks after graduation and I became the "breadwinner" of the family. I took on four jobs to support me and my new husband while he was in dental school. I quickly put on ten pounds and no matter what I tried, I couldn't lose it. I never allowed God to have control over my life. I knew He was there, but I had too much pride to allow humility and grace in.

So, without Him, I became a recluse and depressed. I was working at a job that was wearing me down physically and emotionally. How was I supposed to know that I was harming my adrenal glands and stress response? How was I supposed to know that cutting out carbs in response to gaining weight was actually making me gain more weight?

My struggle with my body image peaked during college, but it began much earlier.

At the age of thirteen, I had my first period, and so began my lovely, messed up cycle. I only had three to four periods a year, but when it came it was like Niagara Falls. I have way too many humiliating stories from high school about my period. After a couple of periods, I began having relentless pain every month. It ended up sending me to the hospital three times in a row.

During the first visit, the doctor in the emergency room at 2 a.m. prescribed me laxatives and said I was constipated. On my second visit, the doctor told me I had appendicitis and the only way to relieve the pain was to remove my appendix. On the third visit, the doctor told me that it actually wasn't appendicitis and my appendix appeared to be in good health – but of course they didn't know that until after they removed it. The ultrasound showed several cysts on my ovaries and one was the size of a softball. Since I wasn't menstruating monthly, these cysts never washed away and stayed on my ovaries to grow and wreak havoc on my body.

I went to the gynecologist for the first time at fifteen years old. The doctors assured me the only cure to these cysts and irregular periods was birth control. I believed them. I was immediately thrown into a whirl of symptoms. It was obvious my body was fighting against me and the medicine.

I gained weight and developed a small amount of hirsutism, which I was told was normal and genetic. I became moody and irrational, and I was no longer fun or happy. I was so confused. I called my doctor at least once a month with concerns that the pill wasn't working only to get two responses: 1) Give it time to work, which usually takes three to six months, and 2) Come in, and we can change your dosage.

I cycled through those two answers until I had been on nine different types of hormonal birth control pills, sending my body through a whirl of changes in a time when my body was already changing so much on its own.

I actually told my doctor that I had Polycystic Ovarian Syndrome (PCOS) on my first visit, but no doctor wants to take advice from a fifteen-year-old. They said not to trust the Internet, that I didn't physically fit the bill, and that I should trust them in the area of my female health. I never brought it up again, but I never forgot about it either.

For those of you that don't know, PCOS is a chronic condition that affects one in every fifteen women. It is a hormonal disorder that causes enlarged ovaries with multiple small cysts on the outsides of the ovaries due to the follicles not maturing into eggs, or lack of ovulation. This may sound simple, but the implications of not ovulating can be overwhelming and severe.

There's acne, weight gain, and abnormal hair growth, as well as hair loss, irregular periods, infertility, depression, anxiety, and intolerance to sugar. It also can lead to bigger issues like diabetes and cancer.

It was the spring of my junior year at Auburn University when I decided to quit birth control. I immediately did a liver cleanse to rid my body of all the built up synthetic hormones. I felt amazing two weeks after getting off the pill. Eventually I started to shed that extra weight, my hair began to grow, my skin cleared, and I finally felt happy. But that happiness was only temporary because it was solely based on how I looked and felt. Everything was great until PCOS began sneaking back in.

I was cheering at Auburn at the time. I had body image issues, but let's be honest, who doesn't at that age. I was so set on staying skinny and getting skinnier that I deprived my body of so many valuable nutrients it needed. I resisted sweets, carbs, and anything I thought would make me gain weight. I was working out nonstop and doing cardio 60–90 minutes a day. I began slowly gaining weight in the middle of football season, which was detrimental to my mental wellbeing.

It was a long vicious cycle of months of intense restrictive dieting, forcing myself to push through long, intense cardio, then bingeing and having no energy to even walk to class. I was supposed to be a happy and healthy cheerleader, and as much as I would pretend to be on the outside, I was crying out for rescue on the inside.

I kept telling myself that it was all because I lacked willpower. I kept blaming my body for not being able to last more than an hour on the elliptical. I was so disconnected from my own body, and I was so lost. My relationship with the Lord was clouded by my struggle to please the world.

February of senior year came around and I was engaged to my high school sweetheart. My fiancé, Will, and I planned to get married in five short months to ensure we were married before he started dental school and moved to Birmingham. My health was put on the back burner and I dove into wedding planning and losing weight and trying to figure out how I was going to handle all the craziness of the next few months.

The pressure just kept piling on. As did the weight. I became super obsessive about my diet and wore myself out trying to workout.

No matter how many times I tried, I could never workout like I used to. My body was screaming at me to stop. But I couldn't stop; I was getting married and I had to look perfect. I tried every trick in the book to lose weight and nothing was working. My focus was selfish and all about the way I looked. I was idolizing my body, and never found comfort there.

My fiancé had also shared concerns about what we would do about sex on the honeymoon considering I wasn't on the pill anymore. I felt a lot of pressure to get back on the pill. Not just from him, but because it was the norm and it seemed like everyone I knew was on it.

My body had had enough of that though, and two weeks after getting back on the pill, I had a panic attack. I almost wrecked my car because I didn't want to get married. I couldn't breathe and I felt like my mind was split into two people arguing back and forth. I was seeing hallucinations, and I thought I was crazy. Praise the good Lord above for my sweet mother who encouraged me – or rather yelled at me – to stop the medicine.

It was a miracle. One day after being off the pills, I was better. No more harmful thoughts, no more split personality, no more anxiety. But it was also two weeks before the wedding and I had just thrown my body into another whirlwind.

One week before the wedding, the seamstress for my dress told me I needed to stop eating until the wedding if I wanted to fit into my dress.

That comment wrecked my world, and I starved that week. By the grace of God, the dress fit and our wedding was a dream.

However, the aftermath of that starvation and exhaustion hit on our wedding night. I fell asleep on the way to our hotel. I got so sick we had to leave at 3 a.m. the next morning just so I could get some medicine before our flight took off. My sweet husband was so patient with me. I pushed my body through the week and ignored more signs it was giving me. We came back from the honeymoon and spent our first month of marriage living two and half hours apart.

I was alone again and still feeling so lost. My body was exhausted and the more I pushed and restricted, the more my body retained weight. I finally moved a month later and the next couple of months would prove to be the hardest I have ever experienced.

I gained fifteen pounds. My hirsutism increased. I was depressed. I had anxiety about seeing anyone I knew. My adrenal glands were fatigued. I was losing my hair. I was getting hormonal acne. My body was desperately trying to get my attention. Little did I know, God was trying for my attention too.

I tried everything else I knew to become healthy again. Even when I was eating healthy and caring for my body, my mind was never fully healed. I was never satisfied. God had to let me lose everything I put my identity in so I could find my identity in Him. I was no longer beautiful according to the world's standards, but I had not changed in the eyes of my Father. I started praying more intentionally, and actively pursued giving it all to Him.

Still, I thought I could control my food and how I cared for my body and just let God take care of changing the way I looked. I had done a lot of research on the effects of food on our bodies especially since most of my work was with terminally- or critically-ill children. I was not eating processed foods and was very aware of what went into my body.

I cooked super healthy meals for me and my husband, and we got an expensive water filter. I thought having control over my food, portions, and cleanliness would fix me. I dove into researching PCOS and was blessed by a family friend for the opportunity to go back to school for holistic health and wellness from the Institute for Integrative Nutrition.

This has been a long, hard process since the majority of the medical world sees pills as the only solution. The more I researched PCOS the more I cared and the more terrified I became reading that it leads to increased chance of breast cancer, which my mother already had, increased risk of endometrial and ovarian cancer, high risk of diabetes, heart attack, and hypertension.

I prayed and prayed that God would show me the best way to heal myself and this is where my story gets better. He healed me. He showed me what He created for my body from the start of creation. He took my worry, took my perfectionism, took my desire to have control. His provision is everywhere — we just need to ask and we shall be given. He took my depression, anxiety, and body image issues, and made me new. God is my Father. I am rescued and redeemed. I am healed and able to do His will. I am His.

He formulated this whole plan for me. As much as I hate every little issue that I had to face, I am so glad to have experienced them all. I know about anxiety and depression, loneliness, eating disorders, obsessive nature, body hatred, hormonal imbalances, inflammation and psoriasis, and weight gain, and I want to help others find their own health. I want others to nurture their bodies and souls with God's love.

God has worked innumerable miracles in me in just a few years and I am so excited to tell of His wonders to everyone I can.

I believe in His miracles and provisions. I will continue to believe and trust in His goodness.

I am finally treating this body as God's holy temple and I fully intend to use it for His good and glory. I am so grateful for the struggles that led me to where God needs me. He is a good, good Father. Now, God has brought me to a place I never dreamed as a possibility. I quit an amazing, stable, and reliable job to follow Him. He had greater plans for me.

I am now working at a studio here in Birmingham called Bloom Studio Birmingham. My job is to teach people about holistic health that points them to our Father in heaven who made it all. I get to shout His praise every day and share my stories with others. God was the first artist. He created foods perfect for nourishing our bodies so we can carry out His will for us. God established rest.

When wondering about the best way to care for your body, look to the One who created it. Look to what He gave us and know that He is the ultimate and sole provider of it all. Praise our Creator not the creation. Praise Him for showing His truths. My earthly father always said, "A job worth doing is a job worth doing right." I finally understand what this means. This is not just our physical labor and what we do, it is why and how we do it. The "worth it" is knowing someone will see Christ through us. This points me to one of my favorite Scriptures, Hebrews 12:11: "No discipline seems pleasant at the time, but painful. Later on, however, it produces a harvest of righteousness and peace for those who have been trained by it."

THE DEVIL IS A LIAR

By Jamie Matthews

For over twenty years I took depression medicine. I'm now fifty-six years old, have been divorced for seventeen years, and have found peace and trust in Christ.

For many years, I was a stay-at-home mom and I would sit at home on the couch zoned out all day. I would be just there. I couldn't clean the house, I couldn't cook, I couldn't do anything. My husband would work all day and then come home and have to take care of all that other stuff because I just couldn't. All I could do was cry, sleep, and eat.

I have lived depressed the majority of my life. I was married to my ex-husband for almost 18 years and my depression continued during the majority of that time too.

I was hospitalized twice, once as an outpatient and once in a hospital.

I knew the in-hospital stay would be tough since I had never spent much time away from my children. I had my first child at twenty-one years old, and he was twelve at the time I was admitted into the hospital.

Knowing I was going to have to stay at the hospital was also hard because the people I encountered there that first day were so hateful. I recall one female employee screaming hatefully at me and telling me to shut up. The male employees looked at me like I was a piece of meat. The patients seemed psychotic not depressed.

I was terrified to stay there. I even thought that I was going to have to kill myself in there, because I couldn't bear to stay.

They ended up letting me see my mother one more time before she left me there. I was sitting in the dayroom crying. When I saw her I absolutely fell to pieces. I begged her not to leave me. I begged and I cried. It was horrible. I believe I had a mental breakdown while I was there at the hospital. Since I expressed suicidal thoughts that day, it is only by the grace of God that I got to leave that hospital with my mother. I was so distraught after that ordeal I took a Valium and it knocked me out for almost a whole day. I was mentally drained. But I never had to spend a night in that hospital.

Shortly after I came home, I was put into an outpatient program in Dothan, Alabama. I went all day for a long time. I don't remember exactly how long anymore, but it was definitely months. I continued to have good days and bad days.

I don't really know what caused my depression. I now believe it was Satan attacking me. But no one knew about my struggle with depression for a long time. I could fool most people because I knew how to put on a fake smile. However, my ex-husband and kids were not fooled. They lived it. They saw firsthand how bad depression really is. They remember me being sad, depressed, fearful, anxious, and over-protective.

For all that time, I had bad panic attacks. I didn't want to go out. I didn't want to see people. I stopped talking to my friends and family.

We didn't have cell phones back then, and my husband would take the children to the grocery store less than a mile from our house. If he was gone longer than I thought he should be, I would call the store and make them page him. I would pace the house. I would have trouble breathing. When he would get home, I would scream and cuss at him.

"What took so long?" I would scream. "Why were you gone so long?"

I had a paralyzing fear of them dying.

I remember praying to God, "If one of them dies, let us all die at the same time." I never wanted to have to deal with losing somebody that I loved.

Back then I loved everyone else first, and I loved God last. I couldn't understand how He could expect me to love Him first. But it's different now. Back then I had no trust in God. It wasn't that I didn't believe in God; it was that I didn't trust Him. I had no relationship with God.

I believe that being depressed is what hell is going to be like, and I have no intention of being there. It's hopeless and helpless. It's mental anguish and torment.

I had suicidal thoughts before going to the hospital. A lot of times I think I would've committed suicide if I hadn't been so scared. I wanted to die, but I didn't have the guts to kill myself.

And there were times I didn't know how I would do it. I wanted to take the easy way out. I wouldn't shoot myself because that seemed too painful. I thought about taking a handful of pills. The only thing that kept me from doing it was my children, because the thought of what it would do to them killed me. I figured my parents and my husband would be okay, but I didn't think my kids would be. My kids would've endured shame and guilt, always wondering if it was their fault.

My dad suffered from depression and drank heavily. I remember being a teenager, and he called me into his room one night, and his gun was lying on the chest of drawers. He told me that if I loved him I would shoot him and kill him. I will never forget that as long as I live. You cannot imagine how much that hurts me to this day. My dad was my idol and my best friend, and he asked me to kill him. People that haven't experienced depression have no idea of the mental torment it brings.

During one part of my life, I worked at a grocery store as a manager, and I would do the new hire orientation classes. I would teach the new employees what I was supposed to teach them for the job, then I would put in my two cents. I would tell them that they should always be nice to everyone, because you never know what could be going on in someone's life. You don't know if one smile, one kind word, or nice gesture can keep somebody holding onto life that day. And you don't know if one ugly or judgmental look can push someone over the edge. It's so important to be nice to people.

I lived in fear for about fifty years of my life. The Bible says we weren't given a spirit of fear, but of power and love and of sound mind (2 Timothy 1:7). I wasn't brought up in church and I didn't know a lot of Scripture. Now if I start to get anxious and fearful, I remind myself of that verse and where that fear comes from because it doesn't come from God.

If it wasn't for God, I wouldn't be here. There were so many times in my life when I was struggling with things — depression and others — that I wanted to throw in the towel. But, God would never let me do it. He would always send someone to help me. He has people to pray for us and believe in us. God helped me through my divorce. He helped me raise my kids as a single mother. There was also one six-month period when I lost my home that my ex-husband was supposed to pay for, I had a transfer with my job, and I found out that my thirteen-year-old daughter was pregnant.

I believe that God allows circumstances in our lives that draw us closer to Him. When we're going through hard times is when we talk to Him more and lean on Him more.

I would go through something and tell God, "If you will help me this time, I'll do better." I would start praying more, reading my Bible, and going to church. I had good intentions, but I would eventually fall back into the same old things.

God is the only one we can put our trust and hope in. The devil is after our faith and he makes things look hopeless, but there is no such thing with God.

In my thirties, I was baptized into the Mormon church. As I went through hardships, I felt drawn back to church. But I didn't feel like the Mormon church was where I needed to go.

My family owns a dry cleaners and laundry business. After my father passed away, I left my job at the grocery store to help my son run my father's business. A lady that worked there started talking to me about God, shared some Scriptures with me, and invited me to her church.

I felt the love of God in that church that day. I couldn't get enough of church so I started going more. I was there every time the doors were open. I started praying more and reading my Bible. Now, I have a real relationship with God. I still work at my family's dry cleaners, and what a blessing it is because every day I get to love on people, talk with them about God, and pray with them.

For the past three years, I have visited a local middle school weekly and talk to the kids about God. I've been on three mission trips to Nicaragua. I teach children's church every Sunday at my church and I do it all for God.

My physical job is still at the dry cleaners, but I also feel like my spiritual job is there too. My job is to talk to people and share God's love with them every day.

Sometimes we feel all alone, like no one understands. But we're not alone. Jesus knows what it's like to feel alone. Remember, God loves you.

The devil tries to make us feel alone and unlovable, but Jesus willingly sacrificed His life for us. God loves us so much that He allowed His Son to die for us. He loves us with a love that never fails. He doesn't love us because of who we are or how we act. He loves us in spite of everything we've ever thought, said, and done.

There are so many people that have never experienced the love of God. There's nothing that He wouldn't do to help us. He wants us to talk to Him and to come to Him. You can't hide anything from Him. He knows it all. He wants a relationship with us. That comes with talking to God and spending time with Him.

I can't begin to tell you how many times in life I have struggled with depression or some other problem, but I assure you I am only here to tell you my story because of God. No amount of depression medicine, drugs, alcohol, food, sex, or anything else can help you overcome the hardships or depression you may face in life. I was on a variety of depression drugs over a span of about twenty years but it was only when I began to draw closer to God that my life began to really change. There is hope, and His name is Jesus. God is fighting for you, just like He fought for me.

The devil is a liar that came to steal, kill, and destroy. Satan makes things look helpless and hopeless. I know how to replace the lies of the devil with the word of God. God's Word will not return void. Instead of rehearsing my problems and the what if's, I cast those cares upon the Lord because He cares for me. Jesus came so we may have life and have it more abundantly. He cares for you. He loves you just as you are with every imperfect thing about you.

What is impossible to man is not impossible with God. Put your hope and trust in Him. When we are weak, He is strong. God can change anything. I know that because God changed me.

I MISS MY CANCER

By Melinda McClendon

While waiting in the car line at my daughter's school, I was passing the time scrolling through Facebook when I read a headline that shook me to my core: "Seven Signs You Have Metastatic Breast Cancer." I was so fixated on the title that I was too afraid to read the article. It took the honk of a horn from the car behind me to resuscitate me.

In 2009, I was diagnosed with Stage 3 B invasive breast cancer. I had two large, lobular-shaped tumors that had remained hidden from traditional imaging, so my annual mammogram, just months before, had appeared clear.

For several months, I'd been experiencing a string of peculiar symptoms and had become addicted to online searches, determined to self-diagnose. Now in hindsight, I realize that I began to fight for my life even before I knew it was in jeopardy.

After an additional mammogram and a second clinical exam from my gynecologist, I was sent home only to binge on Google searches and articles on webmd.com.

It took only two months for a marble-sized nodule to appear in my armpit. Thanks to my friend Google, I was smart enough to know that now, whatever I had, was also invading my lymphatic system.

The surgeon I met with, however, didn't have the same sense of urgency that my husband and I did. Instead, he politely suggested we watch it for a year because it was a very common hormonal event in a woman's life. In fact, his wife had experienced the same thing and after waiting her twelve months, he removed the benign tumor just to ease her mind.

After tremendous pressure from this hard-headed patient and twenty-one days of a strong, unnecessary antibiotic in an attempt to confirm his speculation, my reluctant surgeon took my concerns to heart and performed a lumpectomy "against his better judgment," according to him.

My sweet husband spent the following two weeks praying nonstop for good news. I spent the following two weeks praying for my husband.

The admission of the doctor's oversight wasn't wasted on my ego — I took delight in being able to say, "I told you so." After months of soaking night sweats and a lingering metallic taste in my mouth, I was relieved to finally have a diagnosis that justified my paranoia.

Cancer was like an estranged member of my family. It was that cousin that's discussed in a whisper, the one everyone prays doesn't show up at Thanksgiving or Christmas to ruin it for everybody else. The relative that blows into town, unexpectedly, borrows money, begs to stay on your couch "just for the week" only to steal your grandma's one-of-a-kind heirloom brooch to hock for drug money. Yes, our family tree had a knot in it.

My siblings and I grew up playing in a cemetery on Highway 52 in Dothan, where my brother Danny, is buried. The second of six children, he succumbed to leukemia at just nine years old, a year before I was born. For many years, our Saturday mornings and Sunday afternoons were spent playing hide-and-seek through the neighboring headstones, while my parents cleaned his marker and picked up pine cones from the towering trees on our corner of the property.

To add insult to injury, years later my twenty-six-year-old sister Beth, would be laid to rest right beside him. She, too, had inherited those crazy genes that manifested into leukemia. Cancer and death just seemed to go hand-in-hand in the Sconyers family. It's all I knew. Eventually, it came after me.

I suppose it was because of my family history, but for some reason, my diagnosis never scared me. Ever. Maybe I was naïve or just too dumb to reconcile the facts, but I knew immediately that if God was ready for me to leave this life on earth, it didn't matter what advanced treatment or world-class facility I selected for treatment — if He was coming for me, it didn't matter where I was.

The day the surgeon called with the results, I sat with my husband and we prayed for our family, then for each other. At the time we had four very young children, ages four, seven, nine, and eleven. (And the seven-year-old had Down syndrome). But instead of being filled with fear and anxiety, I had this incredible sense of peace and, dare I say, entitlement. I was confident no matter what my journey would be or how it would end, God had just extended to me a personal invitation to spend some very private, quality, one-on-one time with Him. Just the two of us. How in the world do you decline an offer like that? Simple. You don't. And I didn't.

Not long after Ted and I married, I heard a visiting preacher at our church declare that his No. 1 goal in life was to get to heaven. And his No. 2 goal was to take as many people with him as possible.

I remember thinking that was a great plan and I, too, would consider it my life goal as well. Little did I know that it would take an errant group of cells many years later to put that plan into action as I'd intended. I was determined that in the amount of time I had left on this earth it would be my sole purpose to glorify God through all my trials and triumphs.

So, armed with two poisonous tumors, a bad wig, and a Ziploc bag full of handwritten Bible verses, I set out for my year of treatment with the goal of not simply being cured of my cancer, but to prove to the world that in spite of my circumstances, "I will extol the Lord at all times; His praise will always be on my lips" (Psalm 34:1).

My verse purse, as I called it, went everywhere with me, along with a tiny, hot pink plastic doll from a Burger King Kid's Meal. She stood 3.5 inches high, has yellow pigtails and her little molded hands are stretched straight up as if she's praising God. She became my prayer doll and still serves as a reminder that in all things, good or bad, God deserves the glory.

Ironically, on the day the surgeon called with my diagnosis, I was in bed recuperating from oral surgery I'd had that morning to remove a tooth that was cracked to the jaw bone. The procedure required anesthesia and, once I awoke from the ordeal, I required a handful of prescription pain meds to keep me from gnawing through the packed cotton balls .

If you've ever seen a happy, tipsy person, then you can visualize my aptitude for receiving and responding to the news of my cancer: My tongue was completely numb, my mouth full of gauze and, well, I was in a drug-induced state of euphoria.

As friends began to fill the house and say grace over my defective body, I found myself comforting and consoling them, wiping their tears, hugging their necks, gently rubbing their backs while assuring them it was all going to be okay.

It was right then and there that I realized God had taken over the entire situation. In fact, I believe He orchestrated the untimely oral surgery just to "take the edge off," as they say. God was priming me for my new assignment. He's sneaky that way.

Later that afternoon, still in a medicated stupor, I declined their insistence to create a profile page on a website for people who are sick and need help.

"Those are always so sad," I lamented.

After much debate I compromised on a blog, which at that time was a fairly new concept that was essentially a digital platform for stay-at-home moms to teach their followers how to make curtains out of dish towels and grow succulents in teacups. Though it was way out of my comfort zone, I committed myself to the challenge and "My Cups Runneth Over" was birthed in my kitchen that day.

My concession to write about my cancer was justified by the simplicity of updating friends and family scattered around the country, but void of the sad overtones of the other websites. It was going to be an upbeat, funny, and impersonal rundown of the treatments, types of drugs, wig selection, dietary changes, and biweekly updates on tumor shrinkage.

But boy oh boy, did God have other plans for that blog. It took on a life of its own and turned out to be so much more. Without even realizing what I was doing, it became my very public diary of a beautiful, personal relationship with Jesus Christ and how He and I travelled together during this time in my life.

I had friends and foes reading it and sending me well wishes from all walks of life. Unknowingly, I had invited total strangers from near and far to join me on this magic carpet ride with Jesus.

Suddenly, churches and small groups began asking me to speak to their members; Sunday school classes wanted me to read my blog aloud to their members. And then total strangers started sending messages thanking me for introducing them to my God — some sharing how much my words changed their perception of trials and personal battles in their lives, including their own cancer diagnoses. Somewhere along the way, I recollected that visiting preacher's goals and reconciled that maybe, just maybe, I was delaying No. 1, but hopefully making great progress on No. 2.

The blog became an extension of me and my tumors. But the stories that unfolded weren't about my cancer, but about my journey during my fight with cancer. It was about my family and friends, and how God brought me to this point and stayed with me the entire time.

Months after I finished writing My Cups Runneth Over, I received a request from a national company to advertise their product to my readers in exchange for compensation.

Once the lady convinced me it wasn't a prank call, she recited her sales pitch, then attempted to close the deal by saying the demographics of my readers matched the product customer profile perfectly – whatever that meant.

After a few back and forth questions and explanations, she seemed mystified that I didn't know the analytics of my blog. Nope. I sure didn't. In fact, I'm not even sure if I knew what analytics meant in that context.

Then she went for the juggernaut and asked, "Mrs. McClendon, you do know how many readers you have, right?"

"Well, I have hundreds of friends and dozens of family members spread out over the entire south that were reading my cancer story," I replied.

"Mrs. McClendon, you have readers in seven countries."

I said, "You mean counties, because I definitely have cousins and friends in seven counties."

"No," she said. "Seven countries. Mrs. McClendon, are you still there?" I don't really remember what else she said because by then, my brain had exited the conversation.

After repeating the story to my husband, we both sat quietly, amazed at how diligent, persistent, and adamant God is about spreading His Word of salvation.

Many years later, I'm still blown away by this story, and the reminder that God does in fact, use the most ill-equipped, undeserving, under-qualified, imperfect, unlovable people to experience and spread the gospel. What I can't believe is that He chose me.

During this beautiful time I would swear I could smell his leather sandals during what I called my "nose-to-toes" experiences — those times when we are at the feet of Jesus crying out for mercy (which, by the way, is where He wants us). It's only then, when we're vulnerable and defeated, that we are capable of realizing the magnitude of His presence.

As my treatment ended, so did the blog. My focus switched to my dad's failing health, and I jumped back on the fast track of life as I had known it pre-cancer: my life as a wife and working mom of four.

The trial drug I'd been given had shrunk one tumor by nearly 80% and the other had disappeared completely. After a month of radiation and then, reconstructive surgery, I was considered cancer-free by my doctors at UAB.

My nearly three-year journey back to good health had not simply changed my body. More importantly, it had changed my heart.

When I was first diagnosed, I told my Sunday School class that if God intended for me to live, my veterinarian could remove my tumors and I would survive; if He wants to bring me home, the best oncology surgeon in the world couldn't save me.

I firmly believe that claim still to this day. The advanced cancer, I determined, was simply the vehicle God used to get my attention. He knew my skill set — he created it.

The miracle was not that He saved me, but that He used me, through an errant cell, to further His kingdom. God chose little ole insecure, introverted me to teach people how to love Him through the storm. I know I was hand-picked – the life experiences, the family history, the cemetery, all of it. He had been preparing me for this day since before I was born.

Now, nearly ten years later, I've been able to see my children grow up and my marriage grow deeper. I'm blessed to experience each new stage of their lives — dozens of field trips, two graduations, five proms, and now, two college tuitions. I found delight in teen acne, angst, and puberty— not many moms can say that.

Cancer is my plumb line. Events and circumstances are either ranked above or below. Since then, my dad's Alzheimer's and death have been the only events that I consider equal or above. Otherwise, everything else pales in comparison.

I don't take for granted my many blessings, but there are moments, like reading that random headline on my newsfeed, when a simple word —"metastatic" — puts a choke hold around my neck and reminds me just how vulnerable I am.

It tells me my so-called perfect life could quickly change with one phone call. And in that moment, I long for that incredible time of sharing meaningful and intentional time with God — I long to be spoiled by His attentiveness and His acknowledgment of my faithfulness, digging deeper into His Word and reading Scripture with purpose. I need to need Him more often. In other words, there needs to be more of Him and less of me.

On other days, when I find myself exhausted, frustrated, and feeling defeated living in this chaotic world, I'm forced to admit that, in fact, I miss my cancer. I miss that ability to cast off the mundane distractions and remain laser-focused on God's plan for me and His provisions.

I miss the group prayers from total strangers, the kindness shown to me and my family, the tenderness my husband and I shared, the unity of my friends and foes and, of course, we all miss the food — oh the food.

But more than anything, I miss my sweet time with Jesus. I crave that feeling of being His No. 1 priority, having His undivided attention and He, mine. Unfortunately, it took advanced-stage cancer to unveil what He'd already offered me.

I hope my story encourages you to seek authenticity in your relationship with Jesus Christ. He's waiting on you. He has great plans for my life and yours. Ask yourself, how many souls am I encouraging toward eternal life with our heavenly Father? Don't wait for your cancer; learn from mine.

HURT BY YOUR HERO

By Angela Mitchell

Pain, hurt, helplessness, embarrassment, loneliness, sadness, anger, disbelief. Those emotions are all I felt for years.

Pain because a child who looked up to her father had him hurt her.

Hurt because he did what he did to me.

Helpless because who could I turn to? Who would believe me? He threatened my life and the life of anyone that I told. He even told me that if I had kids he would hunt them down too. How could a loving father say that?

Embarrassment because I knew it was wrong, yet I couldn't say or do anything to stop it. I was stunned because this was actually happening to me. You hear about it happening to others, but you never think it could happen to you. Not by your father. Not by your hero. But I felt like I let it happen; I had a voice, but yet said nothing. I thought of the pain it would cause my mom; I thought of the family it would tear apart. I didn't know how I could talk about it. How could I live like that? With other family members knowing what happened; the looks I would get, the sorrow on their faces, their pity. Maybe even their accusations of me lying about it.

Loneliness because I had to keep it to myself. I had no one I could turn to; my mom was my best friend. I had no one, just a dark abyss that ate at me.

Sadness because I knew I had to stop it. But I didn't know how.

Anger because the man that I loved, that I looked up to my whole life was hurting me.

Disbelief that this was my life – that my perfect life, my Ozzy and Harriet life, my June and Ward Cleaver life had turned into this.

I looked into ways to kill myself, to lessen this pain, and to get rid of the darkness that I was in. To end the abyss of spiraling blackness I was headed for.

I had read my Bible here and there, but we were never much of a church family. I knew it had sayings that would make me feel better at times. When mad I would look at this verse, when lonely I would look at this verse, and so on and so on. It was my salvation only until it got dark again. Until the lights went out. Until I heard my mother's door close and my door creak open. I knew it was just a matter of time before my father came into my room.

"Are you asleep?" Sometimes he would ask. I would try to pretend I was asleep, but even then it didn't matter. I was told I was being taught how to please my future husband. Men did this all the time back in the old days, he would say. Indian men would sometimes let their uncles show the young women how to please her future husband. There was nothing wrong in it, I was told. He told me to just lay back and follow commands, to move more, to not just lie there.

Eventually, I had decided. This was the night. This night I was going to kill myself. I just couldn't take the pain anymore. Nothing was helping. I was sleeping with other guys because hey, I thought that was all I was good for. It's what they wanted. It's how I was loved, how I became popular in high school. Everyone loved me. Who wouldn't?

I remember rolling over to face the wall and crying my eyes out because I just couldn't figure out how I was going to kill myself and not go to hell. I was told if you kill yourself that is where you go. There was no redemption for suicide and I didn't want to burn in hell for eternity. But I was also thinking that it may just be worth it.

Pills were the only way I could see doing it. I didn't like pain and, well, using a knife to slit my wrists would be painful indeed. Pills were an option but how many? I didn't want my stomach pumped if I took the wrong amount and was still hanging on. Then there was the option of speeding and hitting a tree.

I remember thinking, "God please help me, I am so scared to die. I just want to die. God please."

Another day goes by because I am too scared to do what I thought I had to do.

Then I met a guy. A nerd. Someone who I wasn't physically attracted to at all. Someone who when I bent over didn't look my way. A guy who I thought had to have something wrong with him because he didn't even look my way when I crossed my legs and hiked my skirt up farther than it should be. What was up with this guy? Did he not know I was good looking, an easy catch?

He stopped me one day in the copy machine room at work. We both worked at a hospital. He asked me out, and I was too nervous to say no to his face, so I said yes. In my head, I thought I could just tell him no on the phone or just not pick it up when it rang. After all, I was grounded for sneaking out of my bedroom window to go hang out with my friends down the street. Mom and Dad wouldn't allow me to be ungrounded.

The phone rang and his number popped up. I did not answer, but my mom took a message for me that day.

I don't remember much anymore because I have blocked out a lot of memories from prior to meeting this man. But my mother, for some unknown reason (now I realize it was God), told me to go out with this guy and she would handle my dad if he said anything.

This guy came to my house, was polite, sat on the couch, and had a conversation with my parents. He opened my door to his ugly car and took me out. We talked, we laughed, and we both said we were waiting for someone else but that we would be friends.

He paid for my meals. We went to the batting cages and a movie. He was so polite. Every time we got in or out of the car he opened and closed my door. Never did he treat me with disrespect. Never did he try and make a move. How was this possible? Later that night he brought me home, I kissed him goodnight, and closed the back door. I looked up, tears running down my face, and thanked God for this angel. God showed me a way out, He answered my prayers. I knew, I just knew this guy was a gift sent from heaven. The feelings I had of helplessness and despair started to vanquish, or at least I thought. Turns out the curtain was just pulled shut.

Six months later we married, partly for the wrong reasons, but partly not. I did love this man, Todd, and twenty-eight years, five children and two grandchildren later, I still do.

I had two other siblings: my brother and my adopted sister. I was the oldest. Never did I think my father would have done this to my sister. After all, one day I remember telling him to never touch me again and that I would kill him for it. He never did, but that was also shortly after I met my husband. I left my sister in the house with this man. I never knew it would come back and haunt me many, many years later. The pain I have to live with knowing everything that I know now is excruciating.

Eventually, I got a call from my sister, who is now married. She was talking trash about Dad. It makes me mad sometimes, but I understand it.

She said something that gave me pause. I acted like I didn't understand her or what she was saying. It is still foggy in my head to this day. Let's just say my father had done the same things to her, except it was worse: he didn't wait till she was older. No, this sick father of ours started when she was six years old. She was telling me on the phone that she had gone to a counselor and this counselor said she needed to tell our mother.

I went crazy on the phone with her. I was panicked. My mother had no clue. She had no outside job because my father would never allow it.

Her place was at home with the kids cleaning house. She had no job, never went anywhere that was further than thirty minutes away by herself. How could she survive?

"Keep it to yourself," I told my sister. "I did. Look at me. Yes, I have had to go to counseling over it, but look at me now … I am fine ... aren't I?"

But my sister wouldn't stop. She said our mother must be told. It would live in her forever if it didn't come out in the open. She couldn't have kids because of what he had done to her emotionally.

I broke down and I hung up on her. I couldn't handle this. My world was coming to a crashing halt. The life that I had put behind me was coming full force again at me. Why God? Why now? Why do this to my mom? She was fine not knowing. What benefit could there be in telling her now?

I wanted my sister to get over herself. My dad couldn't function as a man anymore, so why tell Mom? Why? There was no need. But it must be told she said. I begged her to let me be the one to tell her. It should be me. I am the one who let this happen. I am the oldest after all. I am the one who will be causing my mother all that pain. I'll be the one to bring her world down upon her because my sister couldn't handle it anymore. So I did.

That day I died even more inside. I broke my mother's heart in a way I don't think anyone else ever could have. The pain came crashing down upon me all over again. Oh the pain.

My mother doesn't believe in God now. She said God would not have let this happen to her girls in her house. You must know the pain I feel inside. The pain I feel knowing that I let this happen to my sister. I told my mom about what he did to us. I sent her world tumbling into that darkness where I had once lived.

One day I hope to bring my mom back to God. The God I know sent me my husband. The God I know has been there in my darkest days, even when I would not allow Him to shine within me. Don't feel sorry for me. For this experience has made me who I am. It has made me strong. This experience led me to the man I love and the children and grandchildren that he gave me.

These experiences helped lead me to Ariton, Alabama, a little town that is just a speck on the map, this little town with an amazing church and an amazing pastor. This experience has led me back to where I should have always been all along: to God. The day I moved here was a day to celebrate. I cannot describe the weight that God has taken off my shoulders. The darkness I once knew is gone.

With God's help, I have forgiven my father … but not forgotten. I can never forget. But I can't hate him. After all, that would only bring me back to where I use to be. I am thankful for everything: life, light, happiness, wonderment, amazing grace, and peace. Thank you, God.

NEVER GIVE UP HOPE

By David Money

Plop, thump, thud, plop, thump, thud. The rubber ball bounced off the chimney, took one hop off the hard, bare ground, and landed solidly into the glove of the eight-year-old boy over and over, hour after hour. His mind's eye saw it as a sharp ground ball hit to Tony Kubek at short, then a quick flip to Bobby Richardson for one, and on to Moose Skowron at first to complete the double play.

This was my daily routine during the hot Alabama summer of 1956. Baseball was my life.

We were poor. Our family of five lived in a four-room house on a dirt road near Shorterville, Alabama in east Henry County, complete with an outhouse and a Sears catalog.

We always took our baths in the late afternoon sunlight beneath a water hose strung over the limb of a Mimosa tree in the side yard. There we were for the entire world to see.

Christmas for my two sisters and me was an apple, an orange, a few peppermints, and a flannel shirt. And, if it had been a good year, maybe we'd get a hand-me-down bike that we all shared. That was country living in rural southeast Alabama — until Daddy lost his job.

He then moved us to Port St. Joe, Florida where he found a job as a truck driver. Mother worked in a box plant. They lived from week to week, paycheck to paycheck.

Saturday nights meant a bonfire on St. Joe Beach, three couples and their kids.

As the oldest child, my job was to leave the fire when one of the adults needed a beer and walk to the ice chest thirty feet from the open fire. I would open a beer with a churchkey and deliver it to whoever had ordered it, sipping the foam off the top of the can on my very slow walk back to the fire.

This was their existence. Work all week, drink beer on the weekends, and hope the money would last from one Friday to the next. Church was never an option for them or us children. My parents' marriage became shaky. I can remember the constant fussing. Fussing that turned to fighting — fighting to the extent that cabinets were overturned and dishes and glasses were broken all over the kitchen. We were frightened and confused. My mother would tell me to go get the neighbors.

Daddy would respond, "Don't you dare move."

My two sisters could only sit on the couch crying, begging me to please do something. I felt helpless. This continued from the summer of 1957 until Christmas of 1958.

I'll never forget walking home from school at lunch on the day before Christmas break in the fourth grade. I was surprised to see Daddy standing by the car. He was never home during the middle of the day. He told my seven-year-old sister, Vickie, and me to get in the car.

When I asked him why, he said, "Don't worry about it, just get in the car. Your clothes are already packed."

No one said anything during the first hour of the drive. Just north of Blountstown, I saw Daddy cry for the first time in my life. He and Mother were getting a divorce.

We moved back to Henry County where Daddy began working for his cousin at a truck stop, which was nothing more than a glorified juke joint.

Vickie, Daddy, and I lived in an old trailer behind that truck stop. He was trying to hold down a job and raise a ten-year-old son and seven-year-old daughter by himself. There were very few rules and no curfew to speak of. We were pretty much on our own.

I can remember walking the grounds late at night looking for not quite empty beer cans and half-smoked cigarettes. Inside the truck stop several tables over in the corner were dedicated to Domino games. Daddy would sometimes leave with a girlfriend and tell me to take over his hand. The wager was $5.00 a game.

There I was, a ten-year-old, drinking, smoking, and gambling with grown men. They were often drunk and I generally won. It never occurred to me then, but now, almost sixty years later, I'm amazed that I didn't end up in some type of detention center. But I'm even more amazed at how God placed key people into my life at just the right time. His timing is always perfect and for me it came in 1959.

Her name was Jeannie. She was sweet, smart, and pretty. I think she kinda liked me…and I was crazy about her. She was also in the sixth grade. We spent many days in the spring of 1960 sitting by a small stream behind that truck stop talking about many different things as we listened to songs by The Everly Brothers, Sam Cooke, and Elvis coming from the jukebox.

Jeannie was an encourager. She told me I could do better, that I could make something of my life. She believed in me. And she proved it with her actions.

Jeannie and her mother invited me to something they called a revival. It was one of those Sunday night through Friday night things that were popular during those times. I remember wearing the same pair of dirty jeans every night. I was embarrassed and hoped nobody noticed.

The last night of that May revival, on Friday the 13th, began a new chapter in my young life. We were on the second row when they sang the closing hymn. I don't recall what it was but I will never forget how I felt. There was a sense of needing to do something, to step out, to go forward. But I held the pew in front of me in a white-knuckle death grip. I could not — would not — turn it loose.

The hymn ended, the benediction was given, and folks began to leave. I continued to stand there, gripping that pew. Then I began to cry. No one noticed, or so I thought. I felt a hand on my shoulder and looked up into the face of a man I didn't know.

"What's wrong, son?" he asked. I told him what I was feeling. He said, "Wait here. I'll be right back."

The man left. I learned later that his name was Calvin Saunders. In a few minutes, Mr. Saunders was back in the sanctuary of First Baptist Church, Abbeville. He brought with him the revival speaker, the music leader, and several others who were still outside. The final stanza was played again. I released my grip on the pew and grabbed on to something life changing.

Almost sixty years later, I clearly see that moment as the turning point in my life. I not only met the living God, but I began to understand how He used, and continues to use, others to guide us through some of the darkest days in our lives.

Later that year, my sister and I were taken in by our elderly grandparents. We were taught discipline, structure, hard work, and the importance of church attendance.

Then as a seventeen year old, He used a Christian coach to persuade me to come to his college to play baseball. Coach Johnny Oppert taught me much more than baseball. He taught me to take full responsibility for my actions, to make good decisions, and to take ownership of my mistakes. And when I had decided to enter the workforce, he insisted instead that I transfer and get my degree.

On a blind date in 1972, I met the girl who would become my wife while I was still a student at the University of Alabama. Early in our marriage, Karen assumed the role as the spiritual leader in our home. She mandated the entire family, including me, be in church every Sunday. I went because she told me I needed to be there, even when I would have much preferred to be playing thirty-six holes of golf with my buddies.

I knew of Jesus but I didn't really know Him. It would be another twenty-seven years until I actually developed a relationship with Christ.

In November of 1999, I was introduced to the Walk to Emmaus. Matt Mobley, a friend half my age, invited me three times to attend a walk at the Big Bend Emmaus Community near Tallahassee. That seventy-two-hour weekend proved to be as much the turning point in my adult life as that revival service almost forty years earlier had been in my youth.

On Saturday night of the Emmaus weekend at Camp Centenary, I saw the face of Jesus and learned, at age fifty-one, what it means to be a disciple of Christ.

Karen and I just celebrated our forty-sixth year of marriage. We have four wonderful children and eight beautiful grandchildren. God has blessed us tremendously. I often wonder where life would have taken me had it not been for folks like Jeannie and her mom, Calvin Saunders, my grandparents, Johnny Oppert, Matt Mobley, and so many others.

My message to others is to never give up hope, to always place your trust in a living and loving God, and to be open to those He will place in your life. You never know when or where it will happen, but be assured that He will always provide you with a turning point.'

LEAP OF FAITH

By Sonny Moore

I joined the Mississippi National Guard on my seventeenth birthday. I raised my right hand and swore to support and defend the Constitution of the United States against all enemies foreign and domestic. I retired from active duty when I was sixty-one years old.

In between those years, I served a total of thirty-four years in uniform, over twenty-six of them active. I served in all the combat arms branches in many different units. Among my assignments were Brigade Chaplain for the 101st Airborne, Division Chaplain in the 82nd Airborne, Cadet Chaplain for the U.S. Military Academy at West Point, Protestant Chaplain at the Army War College, Post Chaplain at Fort Rucker, Alabama, and Command Chaplain for Forces Command Headquarters.

I had many different experiences in many different places across the years. There were many happy times and many sad times.

I went to war and served in a combat zone four times. I have buried more soldiers than I can remember, many dying in our nation's wars. I have often led processions in Arlington National Cemetery, at West Point, or at one of our national cemeteries to lay our heroes to rest.

For a military chaplain, that is a hard, sad, but proud service to perform. I have faced danger and hardship at the sound of guns. I have dug foxholes, traveled through minefields, flown through sandstorms, and endured blazing heat and bone-chilling cold.

I have spent long days with little rest and long nights without sleep. I have slept on the ground for several days at a time and once went three weeks without a shower. I have gone for weeks without a hot meal. Sometimes you look back and wonder why any person would choose such a path in life.

As I look back across my military career, there were many highs and lows, but my greatest challenge came in October 1991. It started with a phone call from the commander of the 82nd Airborne Division at Fort Bragg in North Carolina. He and I served together in the 101st Airborne Division during Operation Desert Storm.

139

The Major General said that he wanted me to come to the 82nd Division to serve as Assistant Division Chaplain. The one hitch was that I had to be airborne qualified, meaning I had to become a trained military parachutist.

He said upon my graduation from Command and General Staff College at Fort Leavenworth, Kansas, he would request temporary duty in route to Fort Benning, Georgia, where I would undergo three weeks of airborne training and then sign in at Fort Bragg.

Airborne school would prove to be the greatest challenge of my military life. The demanding course was divided into three different training weeks. The first week was called "ground week," the second was "tower week," and the third was "jump week."

This course would prove to be my greatest challenge primarily because of my age. The regular cutoff limit for airborne training was thirty-five years old. I was forty-five at the time.

Airborne training is rough on the body. We began each day with exercises and a grueling four-mile run.

The drill sergeants could run like antelope and expected everybody else to keep up. We started out with a class of about 200 and lost about thirty of those guys pretty quick. If you ever fell out of the morning physical fitness run, you were gone. So suffice it to say, the four-mile run was a challenge, but somehow I was able to hang on.

Next were the exercises. Push-ups and sit-ups were a struggle, as well as just about every other exercise they made us do. I think that first week was designed to weed out the weak. It was probably a mental thing as much as a physical thing.

The drill instructors literally pushed us to the limit every day. By the end of the training day, they had extracted every drop of energy that was in my body.

On my first day at airborne school I did more push-ups than I had ever done in a day, but on the second day I did twice that many.

By the end of the day, I was exhausted. I got to the shower as quick as I could and stood in the shower for almost an hour. The hot water felt so good on my sore body and bones.

At the end of my first week, one of my primary drill instructors, who was a staff sergeant, said to me, "Chaplain, you are the worst paratrooper that I have ever seen. If you don't do better next week than you did this week, we are going to send you back and you can start all over."

That struck fear into my mind. First of all, I knew I was not getting any younger and I was probably in the best physical condition I would ever be in. I knew I had just spent the toughest week of my life and was a third of the way to the finish line — too far to turn back or give up. My greatest fear was that I would disappoint the general, my family, and myself. Failure was not a word in my vocabulary.

My class began the second week of training on the "swing-landing trainer." We lined up on a tall platform about twelve feet high. We were strapped, one at a time, into a gizmo that dropped you to the ground as you swung down from the platform. The trick was to make a good parachute landing fall. The perfect landing would be to land with knees and legs locked, turn on one side, and roll. This was the major objective of training in week two.

Each student was graded on each landing fall. As crazy as it sounds, the paratrooper had to have sixteen good landings to complete the training. This training was mandatory for admission to "jump week."

I was one of the first in line to jump that Monday. When it was my time to jump, the drill instructors all held their breath, probably expecting the worst.

As I completed the jump the whole group was amazed and they said, "Chaplain, do that again". And I did. Incredibly, I made all sixteen of my perfect jumps that day. They literally stopped training in all the other lines and came to watch me. I checked off my mission for the whole week in one day, a feat that nobody else in my class accomplished. The sergeants were all excited.

One of them asked me, "Chaplain, what did you do this weekend anyway?"

I replied, "I did what Chaplains do — I did a lot of praying."

The division chaplain for the 82nd Airborne Division at Fort Bragg came to make my first jump with me on Monday of the third week. It was a daytime jump from 2000 feet above the drop zone at Fort Benning.

The division chaplain would be the first jumper that day, and I would be the second, followed by about thirty other paratrooper candidates. I was really pumped up that day and my adrenaline was running higher than it had ever been. We were told that once we hit the ground, we were to gather up our parachutes as fast as possible and then run to the assemble point about a half mile away.

It was a wonderful feeling as I exited that C-130 transport aircraft at 130 miles per hour.

As I jumped out the door, I began counting, "1001, 1002, 1003, 1004," and then I pulled my rip cord to open the parachute over my head. It was a strange, but good feeling, falling from the sky. When I hit the ground, I followed the instructions to double-time to the drop zone.

A paratrooper candidate had to make five successful jumps to graduate and get jump wings pinned on his chest on the last day. The first day was great and ended with me being treated to a steak dinner that evening by the division chaplain. The next day was almost as perfect. My second jump went off without a hitch. The real challenge was on the third day.

The jumpmasters had stressed the importance of "looking them in the eye" when you gave them your static line as you exited the aircraft. On my third jump I looked too long into the jumpmaster's eyes and I held the static line too long. The 130 mph wind took hold of me before I let go of the static line and jerked me out of the aircraft.

Little did I know, I had dislocated my left shoulder. By the time I hit the ground forty-five seconds later I knew something was wrong. The biggest problem when I hit the ground was running off the drop zone. I didn't know how I ever did that — and looking back to this day, I still don't believe I did it. But I did. Just to load up all that gear was challenge enough, much less to run with a packed parachute and reserve chute for half a mile.

I had to do it so the jumpmasters didn't know I was injured. I knew if they discovered I was hurt they would pull me out of the class. The hardest run I ever made was off that drop zone with all that gear.

I still can't believe I did it with my left arm feeling as though it had been jerked loose from my body. But somehow I made it back to the assembly area and caught the bus back to turn in my gear and end the day's training.

That night was another story. I didn't leave my room that night, not even for dinner. I mainly focused on two things — staying under the shower and prayer.

I don't know if I slept at all that Wednesday night because of the pain in my body and the pain in my mind. I knew that the two jumps I needed to graduate were both scheduled for the next day. One was a daytime jump and the other was a night jump. Both jumps would be a challenge. The early morning jump would be my first jump with a thirty-five-pound rucksack, and the nighttime jump would be my first jump into the darkness. Thankfully, it would be a without a rucksack.

That Thursday was a day I will never forget. I measured every step and every movement of my body. I conserved every ounce of strength I had and avoided the use of my shoulder as much as possible.

There was not much I could do about the pain except take some big Motrin horse pills nicknamed "paratrooper candy." Really all I could do that day was suck it up and just grin and bear it. I still don't know how I did it. It had to be my mama's prayers or my guardian angel.

I concealed my injury and limitations as best I could and was able to complete jumps four and five that day. That made better sleep possible that Thursday night. The seventeen days were tough.

Three years earlier, I had completed Air Assault School at Fort Campbell, Kentucky. An article in the *Army Times* said that it was "eleven days in hell." But my seventeen days in Airborne School were more challenging.

My experience was a great example of the power of prayer. There is no way that I could have ever completed this rigorous training apart from the presence of the Lord. I believe that just as He was with the disciples on the Sea of Galilee in the middle of a storm, He was with me in my storm.

I tried to remember three things found in chapter four of Mark's Gospel. Those disciples had the promises of Jesus.

He said, "I will never forsake you or leave you alone." They had the presence of Jesus. He was with them in the boat. And they had the power of Jesus. He spoke to the storm and commanded, "Peace, be still."

I give Him all the praise and glory for anything that I have achieved in life because I know that without Him, I can do nothing.

In Airborne School, I relied on my favorite Old Testament and New Testament passages. My favorite from the Old Testament is Proverbs 3:5–6: "Trust in the Lord with all your heart and lean not on your own understanding; in all your ways submit to Him and He will make your paths straight."

My favorite from the New Testament is Matthew 6:33: "But seek first His kingdom and His righteousness, and all these things will be given to you as well."

A verse I often prayed was Isaiah 26:3: "You will keep in perfect peace those whose minds are steadfast, because they trust in You."

I graduated with my Airborne Class on that Friday morning. Praise the Lord! My story is not one of bravery or courage, but a story of being focused, determined, stubborn, and holding onto Philippians 4:13: "I can do all this through Him who gives me strength."

HE CALLS ME MOM

By Bethany Phillips

Most little girls spend hours playing bride or pushing their little plastic strollers around playing mommy. I was just like those little girls, I dreamed of the very same things.

On a very hot day in August 1990, my dream of marrying Prince Charming came true. Mike was smart, caring, witty, and so very handsome. We quickly settled into married life and began our busy careers living in our quiet little town. We enjoyed being aunts and uncles to our siblings' small children, and would often talk about having children of our own. You see, Mike is an only son, and his father was an only son. The pressure was definitely on to have a boy.

After two years of marriage, we were overjoyed to find out that I was expecting a baby. Our families, friends, and especially my fourth-grade students were so excited. When we went for our first visit, the nurse struggled to find a heartbeat but assured us that this wasn't necessarily something to be alarmed about. On our second visit, however, we learned that no heartbeat was detected and that this pregnancy wasn't meant to be.

I struggled with wondering if there was something I did wrong, and I was determined to make sure it didn't happen again. We were reassured that since I had gotten pregnant once, I could again. These kinds of things happen, we were told, and that after the proper length of time, we could start trying again.

Within a month, we began trying again. During that time, it seemed like everyone around me was getting pregnant. One of my teacher friends became pregnant and came to my classroom crying because she dreaded having to tell me her joyful news. Even two high school students became pregnant, but month after month, nothing happened for me.

I began picking up the mail with apprehension, just knowing that if a small pastel envelope was in the stack, it would mean yet another baby shower invitation requiring me to put on a happy face while inside my heart was breaking.

At school I would find myself dreading going to lunch and having to sit with a table full of teachers, all talking about husbands, formula, diapers, middle-of-the-night feedings, and the war wounds of childbirth. I didn't fault them; it was where they were in their lives. I really believe that God alone gave me the strength to sit there day after day with a smile on my face.

Meanwhile, we continued to try for weeks, months, and even years to add to our family. I would love to say that it didn't put a strain on our marriage, but that wouldn't be true. Getting pregnant almost became an obsession of mine. I was obsessed with being a mom. Thankfully, my brother and his wife had two small children that we showered our affection upon. We went to every ballgame, recital, and party — anything that we could to do to fill the void of not having our own child.

Mike was always wonderfully supportive during this time even though I know he was struggling himself. I researched compulsively, searching for some new drug or process that might lead to our becoming parents. Mike was always willing to research it too, and give it a try whenever possible.

My mom and girlfriends felt so helpless to comfort me in my struggles; several had miscarried, but all eventually had babies afterward.

After nearly ten years of trying, my gynecologist suggested we go to Birmingham, Alabama, and meet with fertility specialists. Finally, I felt like we were going to be getting some answers.

After a series of tests, a course of aggressive fertility treatment was prescribed because by that time I was in my thirties. I was to be given shots in my hips and shots in my stomach – a daily ritual.

It certainly wasn't the highlight of my day, and I know that neither Mike nor my stepmother looked forward to administering them. But I kept telling myself that the end result would be worth it. My hormones began to rage almost uncontrollably, and I would tear up and cry at the smallest little thing.

We attempted IVF; three embryos were harvested, but only one was viable enough to implant. We had no luck.

A follow-up visit with Dr. Kathryn Honea to discuss our next step was scheduled. Mike and I sat down in her office, holding hands and waiting for her to explain our next procedure.

She looked me in the eyes and asked this question: "Bethany, is it that you want to have a baby, because anyone can have a baby, or is it that you want to be a mom?" She told me to sit and think about it for a minute and then answer.

Through tears and around the lump in my throat, I told her "I want to be a mom." She handed us a folder and said she thought the answer to our desires was right in front of us. Now I look back on that day with so much love and admiration for her because her wise words set us on our course to having our forever family.

About a mile or so outside Birmingham, I opened the folder and found it full of information about adoption. This was a subject Mike and I had never even discussed or researched at all. I knew of only two children in our small town who had been adopted, and ironically, I had taught both of them. I knew how desperately their parents had wanted them and how extravagantly they were loved.

We weren't far from home when Mike reached over, took my hand, and said, "I believe that this is the answer we have been looking for." In my heart and soul a sense of peace came over me that I still cannot fully describe; it was like nothing I'd ever felt before. The Lord filled my heart with a new desire, and that was to find my child, my forever child who would call me "Mom."

After much prayer, we decided to go with a facilitating agency. The mounds of paperwork were absolutely daunting. We had total strangers visit our home to make sure we were physically and psychologically prepared to be parents.

Our precious friends and family members wrote dozens of recommendation letters and supported us with their prayers.

The agency even encouraged us to prepare a nursery because many times spur-of-the-moment placements occur. That was such an enjoyable time for me. I was elated to pick out whimsical bedding, a rocking chair, and even a few sweet little outfits.

We were all ready, but where was our baby? Days turned into a month, and then months went by. I have to be honest when I say that I truly started losing faith. My grandmother was our biggest supporter. She would always remind me that good things come to those who believe in the Lord and never waver in their belief.

On a Sunday morning in July 2002, I attended church with my mom. The preacher's message was about faith and the Lord wanting to give us the desires of our hearts. I felt such a burden to go to the altar and pray. I cried out to God, desperately pleading for Him to answer my prayer. A precious lady named Rhonda came and prayed with me. She spoke of my desire to be a mom and that she believed that there was a child out there somewhere for Mike and me. She gave me the biggest hug and reassured me that He was listening.

The third week of August 2002 was just like any other busy back-to-school week in my fourth-grade classroom. I walked my children to the bus and grabbed my purse from the back cabinet. I picked up my cell phone and realized I had a missed call from a number I didn't recognize.

I figured it was just another telemarketer and went on about my afternoon.

It was sometime later that I realized a message had been left and decided to listen. I was shocked to hear our facilitator Diane's voice on the other end of the phone telling me that a birth mother wanted to talk with us and that she thought we would be a perfect match. I tried desperately not to get excited because we previously had a visit with another birth mother fall through.

As soon as I got home, I called Mike and told him what had happened. He reminded me that this was not a sure thing and told me not to get my hopes up too much. But it was already too late.

That evening we received a call that would forever change our lives. A wonderful birth mother had chosen us to be parents to her son. We were going to have a son!

We were told that the baby would be arriving in the next month. I finally felt like I could open the door to the nursery we had decorated over a year earlier. I had closed the door because it was just too painful to look inside the empty room and be reminded that a child should be in that crib and playing with those toys.

My mom and I spent the next weekend buying every single blue outfit we could find. We washed and folded each one and even selected a "Thank Heaven for Little Boys" outfit for our special one to wear home. We made plans to leave on that Thursday and take my mom with us on the long trek to Indiana.

I have never been one to believe in coincidences. I am convinced that all things happen for a reason. We had decided that we would name our little boy Noah. It was an old family name and one I had loved for such a long time.

When we arrived in town, we decided to go to the local Walmart and buy supplies. I heard a mother yell from the next aisle over, "Noah, stop running in this store!" My mom and I just looked at each other and smiled.

We were there bright and early the morning of our little boy's arrival. He was born a few minutes before nine, and we were ushered into the nursery to see him. I know that most parents say their baby is the most beautiful in the world, but I have to declare our Noah truly was. All I could do was look at him and cry.

The ten years of tears, shots, and disappointment all faded in that instant. We had the opportunity to meet Noah's birth mother which was something I admittedly was a little hesitant to do. I am so thankful, though, that I did. I wanted the chance to tell her how much I would always love our sweet Noah. We hugged for a long time, and I promised to always be there for him and love him unconditionally. She acknowledged my promise. She had unselfishly given from her heart the most incredible gift one woman can give another.

That night as I rocked Noah in the hospital nursery, I glanced down at a nameplate on the arm of the chair. I was absolutely stunned. That rocking chair had been donated by a family in memory of their son named Noah. I truly believe the Lord led me to look down so that he could reassure me once more. My long journey was complete. I was finally someone's mom.

That boy is now a teenager and is unequivocally the light in his dad's and my life. We can't imagine what our lives would be like without him.

I have been so blessed to have friends and parents who believed and prayed without ceasing that our prayers would be answered. They were there that day we first drove into our driveway with Noah asleep in his carseat, and they have been there ever since – at every party, awards day, and ballgame.

I often ask Noah if he can hear us cheering for him at ballgames.

He replies, "Mom, everybody in the whole stadium can hear you!" I want him to know that his dad and I will always be the loudest voices in the crowd, the ones that make a thousand embarrassing pictures, and the ones chasing after him with hugs and kisses no matter how old — or how embarrassed — he is.

My prayer is that you can gain some strength or comfort from reading my story. Believe in God's prevenient grace. He does answer prayers. I'm proof of it. One of those answered prayers calls me "Mom."

CHOOSE JOY

By Janice Pitchford

On January 1, 1987, my family was celebrating the New Year in Florida. As my children, Dawn, thirteen, and Jonathan, seven, posed on a sand dune for a picture, I commented to my husband that they were the picture of happy, healthy children. Little did I know that twenty-seven days later I would be standing at Dawn's bedside at Children's Hospital of Alabama as she fought for her life. We had just been given the devastating news that Dawn had a particularly deadly form of leukemia and her prognosis was grave. Our world had been shattered.

Over the course of the next few days there were more tests, invasive and painful procedures, and no good news. Having been a registered nurse for almost twenty years I thought I knew what we were facing, but as it turned out I could only begin to imagine the difficulties that lay ahead.

Dawn had to have surgery to place a device known as a double lumen Hickman catheter into her chest. This device would allow her to receive blood products and chemotherapy at the same time as well as allow access for blood samples. The surgery was to take only forty-five minutes to an hour, but as the hours dragged on she was still in surgery.

Finally, we heard from a surgical nurse that Dawn had experienced a few difficulties during the surgery. The first was because of the disease and the fact that she had been given massive doses of aspirin when they thought her diagnosis was juvenile rheumatoid arthritis and her blood would not clot. They had to give her platelets and fresh frozen plasma to control the bleeding. Then her temperature had spiked to such a level that she had to be given an ice blanket.

The original plan had been to do her first spinal tap while she was under anesthesia, but her condition was so unstable they were unable to proceed with the tap. Finally, she returned to her room with a massive pressure dressing on her chest.

Just a few hours later they were in her room to do the spinal tap. We asked to wait but were told that she couldn't have her first dose of chemotherapy until the spinal tap was done to rule out leukemia cells in the spinal fluid. So the procedure began. Dawn was in terrible pain, weak, and sick, but she had to sit up on the side of the bed and bend forward to expose her back for the spinal puncture.

Her dad and I sat on the floor beneath her and tried to provide both moral and physical support. I could hardly breathe. I just kept telling the Father that I could not do this. I didn't have the strength. I was literally begging Him for mercy. Then it happened.

Never before in my life had I felt the actual physical presence of the Lord, but it was as if His arms enfolded me and He said to me, not audibly, but in my heart ever so real, "I am with you. No matter what comes I will not leave you." A peace and strength came over me that is impossible to describe.

From that day forward I never again felt that I could not go on. I went days without sleep but I never felt my strength give out. I moved forward from day to day and whatever the day brought I had the knowledge that I was not alone.

One day, very near the end, Dawn patted the bed beside her and told her dad that they needed to talk. By this time, she was in intractable pain and nothing they gave her helped. She looked into his eyes and asked him if he could choose to die suddenly and not suffer or to suffer but have time to say goodbye which would he choose.

After a moment to recover and to reflect he very wisely told her that there were good things about both but that if he could choose he would choose to suffer so that he would have time to prepare for heaven, time to tell everyone how much he loved them, and time to say goodbye.

She smiled up at him and said, "Daddy, I would, too." And that's what she did.

At fourteen she prepared to die. She told us that she was ready for heaven and that she was not afraid to die. She wrote notes and made tapes and made sure everyone knew how much she loved them. She said good-bye.

Dawn's condition continued to get worse and she wanted to be back in our home so we made arrangements for her to be taken there. We arrived home around 2:00 p.m. That night, I sat in Dawn's room to eat supper. It was like the first day we brought her home from the hospital as a newborn. We couldn't take our eyes off of her. Our precious daughter was home, in her own bed at last. I was watching every breath. Even then she was beautiful.

As the hours passed her breathing became more and more labored. I told Larry, my husband and Dawn's dad, that I didn't think it could be long. She wasn't requiring the pain medication at all now, which was an ominous sign. Larry and I continued to love on Dawn, hugging her, kissing her, and telling her how much we loved her. Larry and I knelt on either side of her bed, holding her hands she took one last labored breath and departed this world of pain and grief and entered into the arms of Jesus.

On Friday night, September 18, 1987 at 9:10 p.m., Dawn entered her eternal rest. The precious light that brightened so many days and nights for us now shines in another world. She left from her own home, her own room, and her own bed with her dad and me at her bedside.

It was over. Dawn's long, hard fought and courageous battle was over. Her race was finished and she was free. She had finished well.

I wish I could describe how courageous and selfless my child was throughout her battle. During pain that was unrelenting she always, and I mean always, thought of others. I can't count the number of times in her last days that she would put those precious arms around my neck and hold me close and say, "I just love you so very, very much" or she would say, "You'll never know how much I love you." During the last two or three days she would pat my arm or my back and say in her baby talk, "It'll be alright". She was very much aware of what was happening to her. She spoke openly and freely of being ready to get to heaven. Her maturity and strength touched so many lives.

All of her life I had imagined her leaving home. Perhaps she would leave to go to Auburn to attend college. Perhaps she would leave in a gown of white with a handsome young man at her side to bring us grandchildren. Never had I imagined this.

C.S. Lewis once wrote that pain is God's megaphone. I believe He used that megaphone to speak to us through Dawn's pain. Although we prayed ceaselessly throughout the last seven months of her life, God did not choose to heal our daughter on this earth but oh, how He used her. She was an amazing minister to all who came in touch with her. She cared deeply for the needs of others around her and never focused on her own pain. She taught her dad, me, and all of our family both how to live and how to die.

Have you been around people who may have gone through a fiery trial maybe 20 years ago and they are still walking around smelling like smoke? Well, our daughter walked through the fire and she never lost her sweet savor and loving spirit. She never smelled like smoke!

We feel we owe it to her memory to do the same. Oh, don't get me wrong; we miss that sweet girl everyday of our lives, but we have chosen joy over bitterness. Joy at having the privilege of bringing that precious life into the world and joy over the knowledge that we will see her again.

We cannot choose our circumstance in this life, but we can choose our attitude, and we choose joy.

Looking back on those times three decades later I still do not understand it all. I have no answer to why my precious, Jesus loving, kind and gentle little girl had to endure the suffering that she did, but I know this—God does not make any mistakes. He could see the future and He could see the lives she would touch. He has carried us every single day since He took her home and we wait with expectant hope to see her again when we fall at the feet of the King of kings in heaven.

EDITOR'S NOTE — All *text in italics excerpted with permission from Pitchford's book* Finishing Well, *published by Author Academy Elite in 2015.*

LUKE'S LEGACY

By Emily Trammell Richards

I gave my life to Christ at twelve years old, and by all accounts, I was the epitome of a good Christian girl. I worked really hard to win the approval of the adults who watched over me at home, at school, and at church. And it worked.

I was satisfied to live a facade as long as I looked like I had it all together. The only thing that was important was how I was perceived by those around me, not where my heart was.

Until I became a mother.

I will forever remember the moment that my heart changed. I was staring into the eyes of my firstborn baby boy, and I became overwhelmed with the immense love that I had for him.

In that sweet moment between mother and son, God spoke right to my spirit saying, "I love you more." That is when I realized how wrong I had gotten it. I had only wanted to look like I loved Jesus, but from that day forward I was in pursuit of Him.

I began habits people probably always thought I had, but never actually did, like reading my Bible every day and building a prayer life.

Before my oldest was born, Jesus was a stranger. Someone I read about but never actually met. I slowly began the process of building a relationship with Him.

In hindsight, I can see that God was building the roots of my faith. He knew a storm was coming, and He made sure that I was grounded enough to survive it.

Then my middle son was born, and that is where my story takes a tragic turn. Our son, Luke, was born with a urea cycle disorder.

It was a clear December day when we took him to the doctor — Christmas Eve to be exact. Luke was only four days old. Hours before his appointment he had become lethargic, disinterested in nursing, and had a low temperature. The doctors in the office didn't seem too concerned, but they admitted him to the hospital as a precaution. But as

153

soon as the pediatrician at the hospital saw him, he knew something was wrong.

We could tell the doctor was very concerned, but we had no idea what possibilities were running through his head. It had been hours since Luke had opened his eyes and now his breathing had become labored. He was in a coma. Worry was the only emotion I could feel. He had his blood drawn, his urine tested, a spinal tap, anything to diagnose what was happening to his little body. Everything came back normal. Until the doctor tested his ammonia.

When they ran the ammonia test, they realized that he was extremely sick with complications from the disorder that had been wrecking his body since he first began nursing. His ammonia level was over six times the safe level for a newborn baby and he was critical. We had to fly him to Children's Hospital as soon as possible. He had to be placed on extracorporeal membrane oxygenation, a machine that cleans and oxygenates the blood. All the while, it is Christmas Eve and I still have a two-year-old back home.

We made arrangements for our oldest child and made the four-hour trip to Children's Hospital.

It's beautiful how God aligns people to take care of these things when so much is out of your control. I don't remember much about the trip there, but I do remember reading my Bible. The verse I prayed was Psalm 91:4: "He will cover you with His feathers and under His wings you will find refuge; His faithfulness will be your shield and rampart."

"Lord, cover us. Keep us. Heal us," I prayed.

I chose this verse because this is the verse I had written over Luke's door frame in his bedroom. I had no idea how important that verse would become when I chose it for Luke's bedroom, I just knew it was beautiful.

When we arrived, the team working on him was inviting yet cautious. I could tell they wanted me to understand how desperately sick Luke was, but they did a great job of explaining it in a way to help me hold on to hope. In hindsight, I should've seen how delicate the situation was, but my heart refused to believe anything but the best outcome at the time.

After hours of meetings and waiting, they finally got him settled into his room. They had one more procedure to complete, so they told us to go wait in a quiet room down the hall. We were waiting for about five minutes when a nurse knocked on the door.

She came in, held my hand, and told me that my baby was coding. She explained, in the sweetest gentlest tone, that his heart had stopped beating and that they were working very hard to get it back.

Then she said, "I think your baby needs you, Mama."

Luke's dad and I ran to his room and into a sight that still haunts me. Every person in the PICU was working to keep him alive, and they were all failing. Chest compressions, monitors beeping, nurses yelling, doctors thinking. It was a blur of chaos, but all we could do was wait. We waited, hoping for that telltale beep of a normal heart rhythm.

Then the doctor said, "There's nothing else to do. Call it."

And we got nothing. No heartbeat. No gummy baby grins. No skinned knees. No Luke.

You'd think that the moments after the doctors and nurses stopped working on him would be as chaotic for us as the moments before, but they weren't.

The Holy Spirit was evident in that room. That's the only way I can explain the strength it took to hold my baby after he'd taken his last breath. And I did hold him. I held him all the way home. Every second until I gave him to the funeral home attendant. And as I stared into his perfect little face, I prayed that same prayer I had prayed on the way to the hospital but with a very different heart.

"Lord, cover us. Keep us. Heal us."

Jesus was holding me as I held Luke. I felt Him. But the next morning — Christmas morning — I felt nothing but empty. My belly was empty, my arms were empty, even my soul felt empty. I felt abandoned. And I felt that way every single moment until Luke's funeral when God brought me a miracle. It was a small miracle, but a miracle nonetheless. God tends to do that though; he gives you just enough miracles to sustain you. No more, no less.

A friend of mine brought a gift to the graveside service, a gold necklace with a feather on it and Psalm 91:4 on the package. I hadn't told anyone about praying over that verse, yet here she was giving me this gift — of all the gifts she could have chosen. My heart filled with peace.

"You are covered, my child. I still love you more," I heard God whisper.

As we began the process of healing over the next few months, God sent many signs that we were covered. It always seemed to be just enough to sustain us. I told my husband I wanted to plant a magnolia tree in Luke's memory, and two days later there's a magnolia tree on my porch mailed from a cousin in Savannah who had no idea about my conversation with my husband.

My husband, who I prayed would make a public profession of the faith in Jesus he's had for years, finally decided that he wanted to be baptized.

I found a box at a craft store with Psalm 91:4 on it, and it was just large enough for all of Luke's memories. The total at checkout was the exact amount of cash I had in my wallet.

I kept noticing the time 11:11 to a point I couldn't ignore, and my aunt unintentionally led me to Hebrews 11:11 in a conversation.

"And by faith even Sarah, who was past childbearing age, was enabled to bear children because she considered Him faithful who had made the promise," it read.

There were so many little signs, I couldn't help but feel covered, protected, loved. In a season where anyone would expect to feel abandoned, I felt full to the measure of God's love. So full in fact, I wanted above all else to share that love.

As I learned to carry the weight of my grief, I yearned to help others carry the weight of theirs.

2 Corinthians 1:3–5 says, "Praise be to the God and Father of our Lord Jesus Christ, the Father of compassion and the God of all comfort, who comforts us in all our troubles, so that we can comfort those in any trouble with the comfort we ourselves receive from God. For just as we share abundantly in the sufferings of Christ, so also our comfort abounds through Christ."

Through my grief, He gave me a new purpose and the ability to carry it out. Not only did He break my heart for those who are suffering the way we are, He also gave me a testimony to share and comfort them.

My heart still is heavy for the mothers that are praying their babies through long hospital stays. As I drove to work one spring morning after Luke died, God placed the mission of sending care packages to NICU and PICU families on my heart.

After a few hours of excitement and brainstorming, the foundations for what would become a legitimate nonprofit organization was born. Luke's Legacy has helped nearly one hundred families survive a long-term hospital stay with their baby. Some of these babies went home happy and healthy, and some of them went on to heaven long before their parent's hearts were ready.

I have learned so much since Luke died. The most precious lesson I've learned is that no matter where you are, God's not finished with you. He didn't leave me in a cemetery grieving over the death of our sweet baby. He gave me a new song and He gave me a purpose.

Through helping these families, my "Why me?" questions became "Why not me?" I had been blinded by the ease of the world and thought that I deserved for my life to go on as I planned it.

But I've come to realize that we don't get to plan or control anything. We are only to live out the plan God lays ahead of us, and we are to do it in a way that glorifies Him.

For me, for us, that means thanking Him in a cemetery for the few days we had with our Luke, and working hard to let everyone we can reach know that the only way we have been able to survive this world without our baby is by knowing Jesus isn't finished yet. He left the cloth neatly folded when he rose from the tomb. He ascended into heaven to be with the Father, and He's coming back. And oh, what a glorious day that will be.

PRESS PLAY AGAIN

By Becky Stewart

We had a good marriage. Not a perfect one, but a loving relationship with a great foundation based on our love for God and one another.

My husband, Chad, worked hard, so I could be a homemaker. (The term stay-at-home-mom still makes me laugh. It is the exact opposite.) My title came with carrying most of the load of raising our three children, while his head-of-the-household role brought all financial responsibilities, spiritual leadership, head pool cleaner and lawn care manager. He mastered his responsibilities. I was decent at mine. We were content and saw the future as a bright one. Until it wasn't.

My husband died in an accident and our world crumbled.

Several weeks after his death, once the swarm of family and friends left, I purposely went to Walmart and pretended everything was fine. I smiled as I passed people in the aisles.

I replied to the cashier's small talk, "I am fine. How are you?" as she rang up my comfort foods of Coke and Cheetos. It came to a point when I had to stop thinking about myself, about anything, and just live minute to minute just to survive.

My heart was broken. He was gone. Refusing to think about the past or the future, I just wanted to make poppy seed chicken for dinner.

While never officially looking up stages of grief, I am confident I went through the stage of denial.

I felt the most sadness at night, once the kids were all settled and tucked in tight and safe in their beds.

I can remember hugging myself and imagining it being Jesus' arms, thinking, "I need You more now than ever. I cannot do this." I isolated my cries to the shower, face down, water streaming on the back of my head while sitting in the fetal position.

I asked God, "Why, Father, did You let this happen? What do You want me to do next?" Only in retrospect, do you see the sweetness of how close you are to God in the times of grief.

Matthew 11:28 says, "Come to Me, all you who are weary and burdened, and I will give you rest."

For the first few months, I can remember praying and begging God to give me my mission. To not let Chad's death be wasted. I desired to use this tragedy to glorify Him.

Ideas whirled around in my head, but nothing came to the forefront other than "stay the course." I wrote in detail about our last week as a married couple. I sent it to family and friends, and then waited for my next assignment.

I was and still am at a point of not knowing my next steps. This is extremely hard for agenda-pushing types like myself. I prefer to think of my role as God's assistant.

Romans 15:13 states, "May the God of hope fill you with all joy and peace as you trust in Him, so that you may overflow with hope by the power of the Holy Spirit." Trust in Him — I'm repeating it to myself even as I type. I still trust in His plan and have learned so much along the way.

Firsts are harder than seconds, thirds are easier than seconds.

Chad's accident was in April, but our extended family decided it was best to go on an already planned Disney trip in May.

I walked into our hotel room, found a corner, and cried my eyes out. A family trip or holiday is an easy way to come face to face with reality. We learned we had to celebrate anyway.

I find myself doing things for Chad even now. At first there was guilt of experiencing something new without him, then I realized we should honor Chad by living our lives to the fullest.

I had to reset my thought process. When I grieve, I try to think of Chad in heaven. Worshipping at the feet of God, and serving Him in whatever ways possible.

I love him so much, and I try daily to replace my grief with the happiness he is experiencing in heaven.

1 Corinthians 2:9 says, "However, as it is written: 'What no eye has seen, what no ear has heard, and what no human mind has conceived' — the things God has prepared for those who love Him."

Chad gets to be in a place more splendid than my imagination. My heart hurts with every form I fill out as I skip over the father section.

Then my thoughts jump to children that have earthly, but absent fathers, or foster children that have to enter a home of strangers. I wrestle with my thoughts, and I usually win. I refuse to give into the thoughts of what I don't have, and allow the things that I do have to overwhelm my mind.

Although life looks different, I discovered there is joy again. In those first few days after Chad's death, I quickly started sleeping on his side of the bed. I moved my make up to his bathroom mirror, taking up his entire space.

Was it to feel closer to Chad or did I just realize he had taken prime locations in our master suite? I quickly realized that things were going to be different. I was no longer a wife. I was the dreaded head-of-household.

If I could go back in time, an apology is due to Chad. I didn't give him as much respect as he deserved for leading our family. The weight on his shoulders was heavier than I ever imagined. Plus, I hate cleaning the pool, and I am terrible at cutting the grass.

I, however, do a few things different now. Chad liked solitude when it came to our house. I love hosting.

He once offered me a bribe not to have our middle daughter's circus-themed party at our house "because it may rain." I have since hosted a wedding, a couple of surprise parties, countless football gatherings and an annual New Year's Eve party.

Yes, I can picture him shaking his head and saying, "She finally got her way." I have found leading my family is equally hard and rewarding.

1 Thessalonians 5:16–18 tells us, "Rejoice always, pray continually, give thanks in all circumstances, for this is God's will for you in Christ Jesus."

I am the family photographer. On my phone alone there are more than 10,000 photos. One of my favorite pastimes is looking through old photos albums, and those flashbacks on Facebook get me every time. With each picture comes smiles and a flood of memories.

As much as those times are cherished, I have learned to cherish the past, but not live in it. I've learned the importance of experiencing life in the present. I know more vividly than most that life truly is short. This tragedy has molded me into a better version of myself. I just wish Chad was around to see it.

LOST AND FOUND

By Cate Stewart

My family once looked like the kind you see in a ready-made frame from Hobby Lobby. One of those with a mom, a dad, and three blonde children all hugging and laughing.

When I was nine years old, my dad decided to take a position with a law firm in Montgomery, Alabama. I hated that we moved at first. It was hard being the new kid as a painfully shy third grader in a small school.

I was the never-raise-your-hand-even-if-your-life-depended-on-it kind of student. Mix that in with the fact that I wasn't athletic and I didn't have any close friends.

By fifth grade, things started getting better. I had a best friend, discovered I was pretty good at soccer, and for the first time, I made all A's. That year, Dad and I started getting closer. He helped me study and we read together — our favorite was the Half Upon a Time series.

On April 25, 2014, Dad and I went on a field trip to American Village. We were both excited because history was our favorite subject.

Dad had a gentle, easy-going spirit about him. He was smart, but never boastful. He knew the answers to all the history questions the tour guide asked the crowd. But instead of blurting them out, he whispered them in my ear. He didn't care if the group would be impressed he knew the answers. All he cared about was being there with me.

On the way home, we stopped at McDonald's for ice cream. No one enjoys a strawberry milkshake as much as my dad, so of course, he ordered a large. That was the last day I had with him. The last day anyone had with him. He died the next morning.

Losing my dad was hard and terrifying. It still is. His death, however, also made an incredible impact on my life. It ignited my relationship with God.

Originally, I viewed God as this giant, far away King, living in the sky. I went to church and to a Christian school. I knew most of the Bible stories and had plenty of verses memorized.

However, now I realize how personal God is. God is my everything. He is truly my heavenly Father. I love knowing that He is good and will never change. As a believer, there are countless verses that remind me of God's promises of His steadfast love.

John 16:22 says, "So with you: Now is your time of grief, but I will see you again and you will rejoice, and no one will take away your joy." Deuteronomy 31:8 says, "The Lord himself goes before you and will be with you; he will never leave you nor forsake you. Do not be afraid; do not be discouraged."

I clung to the promise of Him taking my sorrows away and replacing them with joy. I try not to fear the unknown because His plan is greater than mine.

It bothered me at first, thinking I was only this close to God because I no longer had a father. I would tearfully reassure God that I would love Him just as much if Dad were here.

I realized that Dad's death wasn't wasted. It was invested in my relationship with Christ. God has given me the insight to joyfully see all the good things that have happened in my life. I have chosen to see what I have instead of what I do not have.

Romans 15:13 says, "May the God of hope fill you with all the joy and peace as you trust in Him, so that you may overflow with hope by the power of the Holy Spirit." I love this verse. The truth behind it is incredible. It motivates me to not wallow in sadness, but to soak in joy.

I have equal emotions of enviousness and happiness when I see a father-daughter relationship. I want my dad and I to share a new memory of a fun trip, birthday, or winning the state championship in soccer. I am left only to imagine his fist joyfully in the air when I graduate college, him walking me down the aisle, or seeing him as Chad-Daddy, his own predetermined grandfather name.

When I fill out parent forms at school, it's still painful to leave the father section blank. For the first few months, I could pretend Dad was on a business trip.

"Coming home soon," I would think.

Then holidays arrived and reality, memories, and emotions flooded in. There seems to still be a missing plate at the table even after four years. No one can really mention Dad by name when we are all together because the pain is still so heavy. Everyone is protecting one another from tears, I guess. Especially as we bless the food, I can hear the quiet sniffles as the room is still and quiet.

Knowing God loves me doesn't protect me from grief or sadness. I still feel awkward, ugly, unwanted, or not good enough at times. The

Lord does guide me back "because I am fearfully and wonderfully made" (Psalm 139:14).

I don't have Dad to tell me how smart and funny I am, but I do have God's Word to assure me I have a purpose: "'For I know the plans I have for you,' declares the Lord, 'Plans to prosper you and not to harm you, plans to give you hope and a future" (Jeremiah 29:11).

Realizing that Jesus understands the pain I feel is so reassuring. I just recently started tenth grade. I am sad knowing it is just another thing my dad will not get to see. God gets that.

Everyone knows John 11:35, which says, "Jesus wept," but I love verse 33: "When Jesus saw her weeping and the Jews who had come along with her also weeping, He was deeply moved in spirit and troubled." This paints a picture of Jesus I forget about at times. He wasn't always stoic and peaceful. He was deeply moved by the Spirit. He hurt when others hurt.

As much as we miss my dad, I can't help to think of his happiness in heaven. He is smiling big that he helped me love the Lord with all my heart.

WHEN IT ALL FALLS APART

By Lisa VanZandt

What do you do when your life falls apart? I asked that question repeatedly in 2014. Up until then, it seemed I had the perfect marriage. But no one knew just how imperfect it was.

With thirty-seven years of marriage, two wonderful children, a sweet angel baby in heaven, one precious grandson, and a job that I loved, all seemed right with my life. My husband and I had the typical marital issues: time management, finances, communication, etc.

Being a preacher's wife, those issues were to be kept private as to spare any embarrassment for the church and our ministry. As a preacher's wife, I could handle these challenges and forgive any minor indiscretions, not because I was a saint, but because of the commitment I made to God, my husband, and my children. Knowing I am an imperfect person and need the grace of God daily, I wanted to extend that grace to others, especially my husband. As in any marriage, people grow, change, and evolve, and my prayer was to do the will of my Father.

In 2011, my husband and I moved to north Alabama to start a new ministry. The work was challenging, yet rewarding. Early in 2012, I began volunteering at a local charity and soon after was hired full time.

As the work at our new church began, we met a family of three that was struggling financially, spiritually, and emotionally. These issues were nothing new to us; we had been in the ministry over twenty-five years and not much surprised us. We both felt the need to help this young family. What we did not know was just how needy they really were. This family had a twelve-year-old daughter who seemed to connect to us.

She loved sports and loved that we did too. We took her under our wing. After a few visits and attempts to guide her, I realized she had more emotional issues than I felt we could handle. She attached herself to my husband in an unhealthy way, and he attached to her in a grandfatherly way, at least at first.

As things progressed through 2013, this attachment began to worry me and I voiced my concerns to both my husband and the girl's parents.

My husband discounted my concerns, siding with the girl and her family, and it soon became a huge conflict in our marriage.

Soon, my husband began changing his own life to resemble more of that of the family that was dominating his life and ministry. Nothing I could do or say persuaded him to distance himself from them.

My husband changed his sleeping habits, the people he hung out with, and the hours he put in at work. He started drinking, smoking, and cursing. He verbally abused me often.

At the mention that he needed to get help, he would go ballistic. He had always struggled with depression and had anger issues, but this felt different to me.

One afternoon, after he had been drinking, he got angry and lost control.

He had never physically abused me, but he was so out of control that day I was terrified of him for the first time in my life. He got in my face, and I asked him to leave the house until he calmed down. He refused, so I threatened to call the police. He then took a swing at me and knocked my computer out of my lap breaking it. At that point, I grabbed my keys and left.

I decided with the personality shift and the suspicions I had about his relationship with this girl and her family I needed to take a stand. We talked, and I told him I would come back if he would see a psychiatrist, stop communicating with the girl, and go to counseling.

After two weeks of separation, he agreed to my conditions and I returned home. I will say he tried to change, but things soon went back to the way they were before. He was constantly on the phone talking and texting with this now fourteen-year-old girl. There were signs that they were involved, but I could have never imagined how involved they were.

In June 2014, sensing nothing would change and escalated anger from my husband, I packed my bags and moved out. The next week I filed for divorce. I knew for my own sanity and spiritual well-being I needed to leave. I am not one to give up on a person or situation. After all, we had been married for thirty-seven years, but I felt God was leading me to distance myself from the situation.

In September 2014, I received a text from a friend saying she was so sorry and that she was praying for the kids and me.

I immediately called her thinking that my husband was injured or injured himself. She told me to turn on the news. When I turned on the news there was my husband being led off in handcuffs. He was being arrested for inappropriate contact with a minor.

Devastation does not even come close to describing all the emotions I felt that afternoon. How could the person I had been married to for so long be the same person that would do this horrible thing? How could this loving father do this to a child? How could a preacher and missionary spend thirty years preaching love, forgiveness, and the consequences of sin, then make such a horrendous decision?

My now ex-husband was sentenced to ten years in prison, and I was sentenced to a life I did not choose.

I was faced with many questions during that time: How do I get through this life by myself? How do I make it financially on my own? How do I help my family come to grips with this new normal? But the biggest question for myself: How do I know if the faith I have in God was mine, or if it was tied to my husband so strongly that it will fail me when I need it most? For thirty-seven years we were hand-in-hand in our love of God, always striving to strengthen that bond together. How could I do this life on my own?

Those questions were Satan's way of entering my thoughts, telling me I was all alone. With the help of God and by His grace, Jesus held my hand day after day.

When I sat on that church pew among 350 other believers feeling all alone, Jesus kept telling me, "I am with you" (Joshua 1:9). He kept telling me, "Lean on me" (Psalm 144:2). He kept telling me, "Take one more step" (James 1:12). He kept telling me, "I have prepared you for this" (Romans 15:4). He kept telling me, "Life is hard but heaven is worth it" (Revelation 21:15–27). He kept telling me, "I love you" (John 3:16).

I am stronger through this struggle because of my knowledge of God. That knowledge brings faith. What Satan intends for bad, God can use for good. I am living proof of that.

My ex-husband asked a question after he was put in prison. He asked, "If God knew this was going to happen, why would he let us move to that city?" I think I understand why.

God was taking care of me. He knew the choices my husband was going to make; he had been going down this dark road for some time. God made sure that I was taken care of. He made sure I was not isolated from my family. He made sure I had a good job and could provide financially for myself. He surrounded me with great Christian friends and all the support I would need to make it.

Is this the life I chose so many years ago? No. But I am blessed. No matter what comes into my life I know my God is here to help me.

I pray for my ex-husband every day. I pray that his heart will be drawn back to God, and that someday he will feel the love that God so generously offers to everyone.

Remember this as you strive to live a Christian life: It may be hard, but I'd rather be close to God through a thousand difficult moments than apart from God in a thousand good ones.

WHEN WE GET TO HEAVEN

By Laura Walker

In writing these pages, I desire to share my dear Alicia with the world. She was only fourteen years old when she left us for heaven.

To say she died sounds so final. I know she is not dead, but living in a better place.

I thank heaven she did not cease to exist, but lives on a higher plain. Of this I am completely assured. She does not live here anymore, but in a glorious place, free from pain and suffering.

It was sometime in the summer of her thirteenth year when Alicia began complaining of pain in her leg. Now, you know as well as I do that children are a complaint a minute, but I knew after a week of Tylenol with no relief something just wasn't right.

I took her to the doctor, who sent her on to an orthopedic specialist. As she lay on the table, squirming from the pain, I grew more and more uneasy. My mother went with us, and when the doctor came in the room and said that he believed Alicia had fibrous dysplasia we were dumbfounded. What is fibrous dysplasia? Were they going to be able to ease her pain?

We left that doctor's office more confused and distraught than before we went. Surely we hadn't come this far to leave with no answers? We brought her home in tremendous pain, and my mother immediately called our family doctor and explained the situation to him. Within hours we were in his office having X-rays and blood tests done to see what was going on. The minute he saw the X-ray, he was making calls to Birmingham and arranging to have her admitted to the hospital there.

In a whirlwind, we were on our way to Birmingham, walking through the hospital doors, and preparing for a biopsy.

Our heads were spinning and my heart was pounding because deep down in my soul I knew everything was about to change. Things like this aren't supposed to happen to Christians who are trying to serve God, trying to do what is right.

I knew the doctor would come out in just a little while, and tell us Alicia was just fine, there was no cause to worry, and it's just a simple thing to fix. I prayed that God would help those doctors to find and fix the problem, and then we would be on our way back to Ariton to continue our lives just like we had been used to.

I don't remember what the hospital looked like, or who the doctor was, or even who was in the room with us, but I do remember the pattern in the carpet. I couldn't look up at the people around me because I was afraid they would see the total panic and fear in my eyes.

I saw the doctor come through the operating room doors and I braced myself for what he was about to say.

His words hit me like a baseball bat. "Your daughter has cancer."

He called it Ewing's sarcoma and the phrase "fifty percent chance" kept ringing in my ears over and over and over.

I stood to my feet and said, "God will see us through this."

Do you know what? I had no idea exactly what it was He would have to see us through when I made that statement. I had no idea just how deadly Ewing's sarcoma was. That fifty percent chance was something I held on to like I was hanging from a ledge.

It's not that I want to cut this story short, but for anyone who has gone through months or years of chemo treatments and radiation treatments, one month looks like all the others: needles, IVs, nurses, doctors, waiting rooms, medicines.

I remember the day Alicia's hair began to fall out. She bravely decided to go ahead and shave what was left.

She was still beautiful to me. I don't think I've ever met a braver person. I am so afraid of needles and doctors, but she never let me see fear. I think she did everything she could to keep us from being afraid.

For sixteen months we traveled to Birmingham and back. I think our car knew the way even without a driver behind the wheel. There really wasn't any way to make this time feel normal, but I tried. If she wanted pizza or a movie to watch while in the hospital, I tried my best to get it for her.

Our neighbors and friends were a blessing. If anyone found out she had a wish they did their best to get it for her. They were always there, always helping. I don't remember buying groceries or washing clothes or doing any of those daily chores that needed doing, but they were always done.

Every scan was nerve-racking. It seemed we lived from scan to scan, and in the early fall of 1995, her scans showed something new.

I remember it like it was yesterday because Hurricane Opal was tearing everything apart in south Alabama, and the doctors in

Birmingham were informing us that Alicia's cancer had started to grow again and had spread to other places. He said they already had used the most powerful drugs and the only thing left would be experimental treatment. Now she was in God's hands. My mother was with us again, and after the doctor walked out of the room, we both crawled up on the bed with her and held each other. I looked up at her and I saw a single tear streaming down her face. One, single tear.

Alicia took her hand and wiped it away and she said, "I want to go home. I don't want to die in a hospital."

That was all she said. After all she had been through, I could not deny her this one wish. But it was absolutely the hardest thing I ever had to do.

I felt like a duck paddling across the water, calm on top of the water but paddling like heck underneath. I have never prayed or pleaded with God harder than I did in those weeks and months. I remember pacing the floor during the night when everyone else was in bed asleep, and lying on the floor, face down, begging for the life of my child.

I never could pray for His will to be done, because I was so afraid that that might mean she couldn't stay here on earth.

It would be a while before I realized that whatever God allows to happen in our lives, faith is believing that it is for our good. No matter what. Even the death of a child.

I wanted to have the faith of a mustard seed. That is all the faith God's Word says we have to have to move any mountain in our way.

I have to confess, I thought if I believed hard enough God could heal Alicia, and that He would.

But the one thing I missed in all of it was the fact that you cannot overlook God's will. It is perfect. Remember, that was the one thing I couldn't pray for. That was the most important lesson, and I missed it.

It was only a couple of weeks before Christmas, and Alicia had become labored in her breathing. Our doctor did a chest X-ray and told us it was in her lungs. Tumors had begun to grow out of her skull. She had quit eating and every day she was wasting away a little more. I simply can't explain what something like that does to a parent. The doctor said he didn't think she would last until Christmas. Even then I held on so tight to the hope that God would turn it all around.

Our house was never empty those last two weeks. People stayed up with her day and night, around the clock, striving to meet her every need.

In the wee hours of the morning on Saturday, December 23, 1995, Alicia decided to go home to heaven.

I remember her grandmother coming in to the bedroom where I was sleeping and saying, "Laura, I think Alicia is going."

I ran to the bedroom and crawled up in the bed with her. She was taking her final breaths and her face was peaceful.

I held her and held her, and all I could pray was "Lord, even now you can intervene. Please, please don't take her, please."

People were all around us and my husband, Dennis, was beside himself with grief. We had signed Do-Not-Resuscitate forms — the hardest thing we ever had to do.

So I said to him, "Come here, there's nothing else to do. Come and sit down here beside her. Don't let her see us frantic."

He sat down on the side of the bed, held her hand, stroked her arm, and said goodbye. I closed her eyes and sang to her. I just knew that angels were in the room with us.

The Bible says in heaven there will be no more tears or sorrows. Thank heaven for that, because I've had my share down here. Alicia is now well and healthy. No more sickness and no more sorrow. I can't wait until we're all together again. I know that it will seem as if we've never been apart. No one escapes life unscathed. Everyone faces tragedy. Through our darkest hour, God showed His steadfast love.

If I could say something to another mother or father who is going through what we've been through, it would be to never waver in your faith. Trust without a doubt that God has your best interest at heart. Know that His will is the only thing that is perfect and it will be the best thing for you. No matter what. I believe that God teaches and refines us through pain and suffering.

Romans 8:28 says, "And we know that in all things God works for the good of those who love him, who have been called according to his purpose." Alicia had the faith to know that even if He didn't heal her here He would take care of her. From that she never wavered.

The story of Alicia's sickness would not be complete if it were to stop with her passing. There's so very much more to tell about this, but it is a very personal story.

I guess I should begin on the day she left us. As soon as word got around that she had died, our house was full of people. Even more than was normal for the few weeks before.

People were coming in and out of the bedroom. Each person searching for some way to help in such a helpless situation. I knew the funeral director would be coming soon to pick her up, and those moments before that were precious to me.

When the funeral director arrived, I told him that I wanted to be the one who put on her makeup and fixed her hair. It brought me great peace to be able to have that special memory with her.

Our house was never empty. Hundreds of people came to our home and to her funeral. We could not believe that we had so many wonderful friends.

She died the day before Christmas Eve and we buried her the day after Christmas. That was the strangest and saddest Christmas we have ever experienced.

It didn't take long for reality to set in after the funeral. I have always said people are so good to be there for you while the funeral is going on, but after the service is over people go back to their lives. They return to their normal routines, not dwelling on the fact that your normal has been ripped to shreds.

Some of the relatives had taken our other two kids home with them, and it left a very lonely house for me and Dennis. Every corner seemed dark and empty, and it groaned from the loneliness of it all.

Now, I'm going to admit something at the time I would have done anything to hide from other people.

After I realized that the funeral home wasn't going to call me, tell me that Alicia had miraculously sat up, started talking, and this was all a big mistake, and God's answer to her healing was, "No, not here," I began to feel betrayed.

I was angry and I found myself saying, "I cannot believe this is happening to me."

It was extremely hard for Dennis during this time. I know that he was dealing with his own loss in the only way he knew how. He's always been the type person that holds his feelings inside, and you don't always know what he is thinking or how he is feeling. But I knew. I knew that the same pain that was stabbing me in the chest was stabbing him too.

I have to be truthful when I say that I was angry at God for not answering my prayers in the way I felt He should have.

I was Alicia's mother. No one could take care of her better that I could. They say time heals all wounds, but two years after we lost Alicia, I was still at a place where sorrow constantly held my hand. I was upset, and really didn't care to get over it quickly.

I had never lost a child before, so I didn't exactly have a manual to tell me how I was supposed to handle it. My winging it did not work, and I'll tell you it is awfully hard to pray to someone you're angry with.

Now, some people might gasp when they hear me say, "I'm angry with God," but I'm here today to tell you that there is not one emotion that God does not understand. He knows anger, hurt, disappointment, heartache, loss. He knew what I was going through even before I knew what I was going through.

I remember so vividly the day I call my "nervous breakdown day" and "my glorious breakthrough day." It was the day I finally realized if I wanted my heart to be whole again, I could not keep this attitude toward God. I went for a walk in those Barbour County woods and I told God that I was going to keep walking until I had the answer for all the questions that had burdened me for three years. I prayed and I walked, and I walked and I prayed.

I know exactly where I was standing when that still, small voice spoke what I needed to hear. It stopped me dead in my tracks.

It said, "I don't have to explain anything to you." At that moment I realized just how small and insignificant I really was. Was I shaking my fist at the Almighty God? He let me know that I didn't have to know all the answers, but if I loved Him like I said I did, I had to trust Him.

If what we went through in losing our precious Alicia wasn't what you would call a "trial by fire" experience, then I honestly cannot imagine what such an experience would entail. It felt like I was poured into the furnace to burn off things that didn't need to be there, like a tree that was pruned of unnecessary branches. I felt whittled. Thank God for whittling me.

There was a time when I thought I would never know joy again. Losing a child is like having a part of you cut off with no anesthesia. It is pain like no other pain. I have lost loved ones in my life. Cousins, grandparents, aunts, uncles, my mother, my father-in-law. But as painful as all those were, it simply cannot compare to the pain of losing a child. Until you have walked in the shoes of someone who has been there, you just can't understand.

I believe that God allows us to go through things in our lives so when we see someone else going through that, we can go to them, put our arms around them, and say, "I know what you are going through, and I'm praying for you."

I wish that I had done things differently in looking back at my life. I wish I had trusted more and leaned on my own understanding less. I wish I wouldn't have cared as much about what other people thought about my faith, and actually confessed what I was struggling with. I wish I hadn't let Satan blind me to the fact that God always had my best interest at heart. Or let him make me think that I was the only one who had ever suffered in such a horrible way. I realize, just like the children of Israel, I wandered in the wilderness way longer that I should have, because I kept feeling sorry for myself.

If God works all things for the good of those who love Him, then I have to believe that includes losing precious loved ones.

My healing didn't come until I realized that one special word. All.

I had not given God my all. All included my children. We sing the song, "All to Jesus, I Surrender," but I think sometimes we don't really know what that means. Sure, God can have some of my money, my time, my talents, but everything? Even my family? Even my children? That, my friends, is true surrender.

All the time I thought God had turned His back on me, I realize I was the one who walked away. He had never moved.

Today I am safe once more in His arms, and I know beyond a shadow of a doubt that I will see my Alicia again one day. We will have eternity to share together. I thank God for His mercy and His loving kindness and for standing there, waiting patiently for me to come home.

WHO WE SERVE

By Dave Walsh

Growing up in the Detroit area in an upper middle-class family, I always expected my life to be fairly predictable: go to college, get married, start a family, join a company, and start the climb up the corporate ladder.

Somehow, I managed to mess that plan up. Instead of a company, I went into the classroom to teach English and read to a bunch of teenagers who didn't have any desire to learn what I was trying to teach them.

After a few years of beating my head against the wall day after day, I actually made the jump into the corporate world as a salesman for a yearbook publishing company. Three years of that was more than I could handle, so I began working for a local printer and then an independent phonebook publisher.

Each time I made a career change, my perceived instability caused my parents, my in-laws and, probably, my wife Tracy, a considerable amount of concern and consternation.

"When are you going to settle on something?" "What are you doing this week?" "Do we still have a roof over your heads?"

These were just some of the questions that worked their way into most conversations at one point of another.

Along this rollercoaster ride of job changes, another change came into my life. Growing up, we never went to church much. We'd go to the occasional Easter or Christmas service, but not much more often.

After our fourth move and our second child, we moved to a small town with few opportunities to meet new people. One activity available was tennis, which had no attraction to this couch potato.

The other was to go to church, so we started to go on a regular basis. While at this church and through the influence of some other people we met along the way, both my wife and I came to a saving knowledge of Jesus Christ.

At the time, we thought this decision was important from an eternal perspective, but we had no idea of the impact it would have in our lives.

175

Shortly after my salvation, I actually spoke in church on several occasions — but I will not call it preaching due to the pained looks on the congregation's faces. We were serving the Lord and growing in the faith.

During this exciting time of spiritual growth, our family grew as well. Two years after our second child was born, another girl came along. Eighteen months later, our fourth child, another girl was born. We now had one son and three daughters.

This was a difficult time for us since we had no insurance to cover the pregnancies and births of our last two children. We had to pay out-of-pocket which put us in a very difficult financial bind. There was no way to pay off the debt quickly, and we barely seemed to be keeping our heads above water.

One day, a man who we barely knew came up to us and said, "I think you have some serious financial concerns." We admitted that we did and, over the course of the next few weeks, he counselled us on the biblical way to view money and finances, and he gave us some strategies to dig our way out of debt.

Over the next three years, we began our climb out of debt. We were making some serious strides in the right direction when God's call came that changed the direction of our lives.

Not long after our salvation, we moved to another church where we felt we could be better fed (spiritually, I mean, not in the Baptist sense of casserole dishes). At this church I began working with the youth on Sunday afternoons, and eventually was asked to be the part-time youth pastor. I accepted and for the next six years, I served in that capacity with a successful and growing youth group.

This new venture was met with raised eyebrows and strange questions from family members. Since I was still working a regular full-time job, everyone was okay with this 'hobby' of mine. But God was not done with me yet.

Toward the end of my time as a part-time youth pastor, I felt the calling to do more. I prayed and prayed, my wife prayed and prayed, our friends prayed and prayed as well. We all felt God was calling me into full-time pastoral ministry.

After my wife and our closest friends came into agreement with the direction of my future — they were excited, but I was feeling nauseous about it — I called up the former music minister at our church who had moved to Alabama to a new church. I told him where we thought God was leading me and my family.

He said one thing, "Send me a resume." I did, but I didn't think much more about it.

A couple of weeks later, I was driving home from a photo shoot. On that ride, I kept seeing church after church and house after house.

When I got home to my double-wide trailer, I told my wife, "I want a church to pastor and a house to live in.

She said, "Why don't you pray about it." Don't you hate it when your spouse states the obvious? I sat down right then and there and started praying. About an hour later, I was called to supper and just after I sat down, the phone rang. It was the director of missions for an association of Baptist churches in Alabama.

He said, "I have a church that has looked at your resume and is interested in talking to you about being their pastor. Can I have them call you?"

After a moment of stunned silence, I said yes. Moments later the chairperson of the search committee called and we set up a time for me to meet with the committee and preach at the church.

My wife and I made the seven-hour drive to UCLA (Upper Corner of Lower Alabama), and had a great time meeting the committee and preaching to that church.

Before I continue, since I wanted to be completely certain as to God's calling of me into full-time ministry and to Alabama, I had laid out three figurative fleeces of wool that had to be met for me to know this calling was from God. The first was that we needed a four-bedroom house for our family of six. The second was that the house needed to be in a neighborhood so the kids would have a safe place to ride bikes and play. The third was that I needed a shop since I was into construction and woodworking. As an additional request, I asked God if there could be a pond or lake close by since I have always loved being around water.

After having lunch with the search committee, we asked if we could see the church and the pastorium. As we were driving to the pastorium, I asked if it was in a neighborhood. I was told it was. *Check.*

I asked how many bedrooms the house had. They told me it had four. *Double check.*

I then asked if it had a shop. They said, "Of course it does." *The trifecta.*

Just to be thorough, I asked, "I don't suppose there's a pond close by?"

They said, "Liza's Pond is just two blocks away." *Bingo.*

As we pulled into the neighborhood we were expecting something out of "Leave It To Beaver." Instead it was a slag road with about twenty houses and trailers scattered about. We pulled up to a small frame house that was a bit less majestic than we had planned on, but there were four bedrooms, although the smallest one could also be classified as a walk-in closet.

I looked out the side window to check out the shop. It was a 12' x 12' shed, but it was a shop.

I didn't bother to look at the pond, assuming it would be pristine with a rope swing and a little beach area. I later found out the pond was covered with duckweed and was home to a twelve-foot alligator. But it was a pond. This all just proves that one should be very specific in their prayer requests … I kid.

When we visited the church, we immediately fell in love with the spirit in the place. We felt confident this was where we were called to serve. That is until they wanted to talk salary.

Now, remember, we were a family of six. Money was not a big motivator to me, but we did need enough to survive. When they told us what they would offer, both my wife and I quit breathing for a while. It was only slightly more than half what we were currently making. Fortunately, God kept us from fainting or running out of the church. Instead, we said we'd have to pray about it and let them know.

On the way back home, Tracy and I prayed and discussed it and prayed some more and we came to the conclusion that if God had brought us this far and satisfied all of my "fleeces of wool," we needed to take a step of faith and trust God. We called the search committee chairperson and told her that the salary was not an issue should the church call us.

Amazingly, we received a call the next night informing us the finance committee at the church had met and decided to increase the salary by fifty percent. It still was less than we were making, but it was enough. God handled the situation without a hitch. All He wanted from us was a little bit of faith.

To make a long story short, I was called to be their pastor a few weeks later. We were elated.

As we accepted the call to move to Alabama, one of our goals was to pay off our outstanding debts and begin our ministry in a better financial standing. The problem was, we still had a long way to go. As we were praying about this, my employer came up to me and asked if I wanted to sell our double-wide trailer since it was on the edge of their farmland and it could be of use to them. The amount they paid was both enough to pay off the mortgage and pay almost all of our debt. To God be the glory! We still owed for our cars, but everything else was under control.

We were elated to be heading out to our new missions field. Our friends were sad to see us move, but they were proud that we were answering God's call. Everything was going great, until we broke the news to our families.

To say that our big news was met with less-than-enthusiastic responses would be a major understatement.

The comments ranged from, "Are you crazy?" to "Alabama? No one moves *to* Alabama!" to "Y'all are going to starve going into the ministry."

It was devastating to hear those comments and to feel so unsupported in a decision we had thought about, prayed about, and struggled with for such a long time. We questioned ourselves, we questioned God, but in the end, we knew that God had called us into this.

So we moved to Alabama, and we have been in full-time ministry for twenty years.

Eventually, our families came to realize the calling was for real.

I even heard the words, "I am proud of you, son," from my father.

The moral of this story is that we all serve Someone much bigger than us, and that Someone is God and His Son under the power of the Holy Spirit. We need the support of our friends and our family, but at the end of the day, it's what God tells us to do that is of supreme importance.

Trusting Him to change the direction of my life, trusting Him to move us to a foreign land, and trusting Him to put me in a place and a position that I could only succeed in by His grace and mercy are the greatest decisions I have ever made. Never be afraid to trust the God who created each of us and who knows us better than we know ourselves.

Remember these verses when you are struggling with something God is calling you to do:

- Philippians 4:13: "I can do all things through Christ who gives me strength."
- Jeremiah 29:11: " 'For I know the plans I have for you,' declares the Lord, 'Plans to prosper you and not to harm you, plans to give you hope and a future.' "

TO GOD ALONE BE THE GLORY

By Maggie Walsh

There's nothing quite like small town living. Everyone knows your name, or at least who you're related to, and all it takes is one great game, one big performance to get famous within your city limits. There are countless pros and cons to small town life, and I could talk about them for hours, but one of the cons that I know intimately is this: Everyone knows when you fail.

Up until my senior year of high school, I didn't really know failure. Failure and I weren't friends, and I had no intention of becoming friends … ever. Sure, I had some disappointments in my short seventeen years, but I was living quite comfortably on my high horse.

Pride was my step stool, and each good grade, each time I compared myself to another and thought, "I would never make that mistake," another step was added. And sitting astride my high horse at what felt like a great height, it just made sense to me that "shooting for the stars" would be easy enough — just lob an arrow up a little and voila! Goal achieved!

So I grabbed an arrow, lined up my shot, and let go. And as the arrow whizzed through the air, I began to get excited. The trajectory looked perfect. The anticipation of actually winning began to well up in my chest, making my breath come out in shallow, fast bursts. Then, at the last minute, the arrow began to drop. Its descent was fast, decisive. Within moments, it was out of sight. The silence that followed was oppressive and frightening. I had missed the mark. What now?

I remember my father walking down the driveway toward me, holding an envelope in the air, the rest of the day's mail tucked under his other arm. I took a few quick steps, excitement making my movements jerkier than they would normally be. I had been waiting for this letter for months. After countless doctor's appointments, recommendation letters, essays — so many hoops just to meet their requirements and prove my worth to them, finally I would know for sure.

Becoming a pilot was the only real dream I'd ever had and getting accepted into the U.S. Air Force Academy in Colorado was how I was going to make it happen. If I was going to be a pilot, I wanted to be the best. That meant going to the Academy.

As my hands wrapped around the thin envelope, my focus narrowed. All I could see was the embossed return address and my full name on the front. I tore into the envelope feverishly because waiting another second was pure torment. I had to know. As I quickly unfolded the plain paper, my heartbeat thumped loudly in my ears. My eyes scanned the introduction and halted on the first sentence. I don't even remember the exact wording, but I remember I stopped reading. Suddenly everything was quiet — even the air was still. The meaning of the words I saw began to sink in. I didn't get in.

I heard a loud sob and didn't even realize I was the source of the sound until I felt the tears streaming down my face. I saw my father wrap his arms around me, but I didn't feel the pressure of his hug. The numbness of shock had already permeated my entire body, and I was just a vessel for the pain that was beginning to roil inside of me.

I don't remember taking a step, walking inside, passing by the rest of my family. All I remember is letting the blue cotton of my pillowcase absorb the flood of tears I couldn't seem to stop. One by one, family members came in and sat with me. They held my hand and rubbed my back. Few words were said, but I can still see their faces mirroring my own sorrow and helplessness to do anything to change what had just happened. Looking back now, I realize that I did more than put all my cards on the long shot by betting on the Academy. I unintentionally placed my identity in a future I felt increasingly sure I was going to step into. So when I opened the envelope with my name printed on it, I was opening who I was going to become.

In chasing my dream of going to the Academy, I had subconsciously placed all my hope in an outcome. And when that envelope bearing my name held rejection, I took on the identity of a failure. It was a weight on my heart and the gnawing thought in the back of my mind.

"You failed. Now who are you? Everyone knows, and they're talking about it. Not so high and mighty now, are you?"

The thoughts haunted me, striking when I laid in my bed each night, begging God for a slumber that was more elusive than the answer to the one question I had for Him: "Why?"

Why would He put this dream in my heart and head, only to rip it away at the last minute? If I'm being honest, I still wrestle with this question on occasion. I truly have no idea why this was one of the avenues God led me down in order to bring me closer to Him. I would have chosen a different path.

But He is sovereign.

If I had gone to the Academy, I never would have gone to Troy University. I wouldn't have majored in journalism, and I wouldn't have traveled the country giving character-building presentations to students.

I never would've taken a job at a newspaper in Birmingham, and I wouldn't have met the people who have challenged my faith, invited me into community and loved me through some of the hardest years of my life — the twenties.

I wouldn't be the person I am today if I had gone to the Academy. And I wouldn't know and trust the character of God if I hadn't experienced the pain and shame of failure.

God had to bring me low in order to build me up. There's still so much work to do, so much refining fire to come. But He is a faithful Father who loves us enough to want His best for us, not just our personal plans and finite goals.

Most days I'm thankful for my first big failure. Its lessons cut deep, exposing the darkest parts of my heart to the light of God's grace. That light changed me.

So on the days when I don't feel the light, days when the darkness seems to win, I rest in the knowledge that my feelings do not define my reality. The truth of my God and His gospel is greater than my circumstances, my perspective, my preferences, and my sin-soaked heart.

Soli deo gloria — to God alone be the glory.

INDEX

50599799R00119

Made in the USA
Lexington, KY
29 August 2019